Sir Henry Morton Stanley, Confederate

Sir Henry Morton Stanley

CONFEDERATE

Edited, with an Introduction, by
Nathaniel Cheairs Hughes, Jr.

Louisiana State University Press   *Baton Rouge*

MM

Copyright © 2000 by Louisiana State University Press
All rights reserved
Manufactured in the United States of America
First printing
09 08 07 06 05 04 03 02 01 00
5 4 3 2 1

Designer: Barbara Neely Bourgoyne
Typeface: Janson Text
Typesetter: Coghill Composition, Inc.
Printer and binder: Thomson-Shore, Inc.

Library of Congress Cataloging-in-Publication Data

Stanley, Henry M. (Henry Morton), 1841–1904.
    Sir Henry Morton Stanley, confederate / edited, with an introduction, by Nathaniel
Cheairs Hughes, Jr.
        p. cm.
    Includes bibliographical references and index.
    ISBN 0-8071-2587-3 (cloth : alk. paper)
    1. Stanley, Henry M. (Henry Morton), 1841–1904. 2. United
States—History—Civil War, 1861–1865—Personal narratives,
Confederate. 3. United States—History—Civil War, 1861–1865—Personal
narratives. 4. Arkansas—History—Civil War, 1861–1865—Personal
narratives. 5. Illinois—History—Civil War, 1861–1865—Personal
narratives. 6. Prisoners of war—Illinois—Camp Douglas—Biography. 7. Camp
Douglas (Ill.)—Biography. 8. United States—History—Civil War,
1861–1865—Naval operations. 9. Sailors—United States—Biography. 10. Shiloh,
Battle of, 1862—Personal narratives. I. Hughes, Nathaniel Cheairs. II. Title.

E605.S82 2000
973.7'82—dc21   00-038452

All photographs are reprinted from *The Autobiography of Sir Henry Morton Stanley*, edited
by Dorothy T. Stanley (New York: Houghton Mifflin, 1909).

The paper in this book meets the guidelines for permanence and durability of the
Committee on Production Guidelines for Book Longevity of the Council on Library
Resources. ∞

For
Adam, Scott, Nathan, and David

with the hope
that Stanley may touch them

Contents

Illustrations

Acknowledgments

It is a pleasure to recognize and thank those who have helped me so graciously with this project: Bruce S. Allardice, Des Plaines, Illinois; Tito Brin, New Orleans Public Library; Robert S. Davis, Hanceville, Alabama; Mary Lou Eichhorn, Historic New Orleans Collection; John L. Ferguson, Arkansas Historical Commission, Little Rock, Arkansas; Robert I. Girardi, Chicago, Illinois; Robert E. L. Krick, Richmond, Virginia; Michael P. Musick, National Archives, Washington, D.C.; James H. Ogden III, Chickamauga-Chattanooga NMP, Fort Oglethorpe, Georgia; Peter Snyder, Ringgold, Georgia; Julie Thomas, Chicago Historical Society; and Dewitt Yingling, Beebe, Arkansas.

I appreciate the work of my copy editor, Andrea Blair, who displayed patience, exactitude, and a friendly spirit.

As always, I am deeply indebted to my wife, Bucky, who, as an act of love for me, has invested much of herself in Henry Morton Stanley. I am obligated, too, to the boys and girls of the Ann Garber Elementary School who showed me the way.

Chattanooga, Tennessee
New Year's Eve, 1998

Abbreviations Used in Notes

General

HH	Household
CSR	Compiled Service Record
DTS	Lady Dorothy Tennant Stanley
HHS	Henry Hope Stanley
HMS	Sir Henry Morton Stanley
RG	Record Group

Repositories

NA	National Archives, Washington, D.C.

Books, Periodicals, and Documents

B&L	*Battles and Leaders of the Civil War*
CV	*Confederate Veteran*
OR	*The War of the Rebellion: A Compilation of the Official Records of the Union and Confederate Armies.* Unless otherwise indicated, all volumes cited throughout the notes are from Series I.
OR Supp.	*Supplement to the Official Records of the Union and Confederate Armies*

Sir Henry Morton Stanley, Confederate

Introduction

I came to Sir Henry Morton Stanley's *Autobiography* as a young man, preparing the biography of William J. Hardee. I discovered it deep in the stacks of the Wilson Library at the University of North Carolina on a day, I believe, when I was tired, when I had broken away from poring through what seemed endless pages of the *Official Records of the Union and Confederate Armies*. Finding Stanley proved one of those happy accidents that sometimes occur in research. I had pulled the volume off the shelf and was idly leafing through the pages when the chapter title "Shiloh" caught my eye. I was astonished—Stanley had been a Confederate soldier. I didn't know that. I read on. I thought his account of Shiloh splendid. I still do. It has a fresh yet surreal feel that seems quite contemporary, and reminds one of Stephen Crane.

Thirty years later I returned to Stanley's autobiography when writing the story of the Battle of Belmont. Stanley had been there too— November 7, 1861—watching the fighting from atop the white chalk bluffs at Columbus, Kentucky. Once again, I was impressed by the clarity and beauty and accuracy of his account. I included it happily.

More recently, as an old man, I had occasion to talk to a group of boys and girls in an inner-city school here in Chattanooga. I had planned reading to them, and, as I rode out to the school, in the seat beside me I carried reading material—something from Ranger Rick suggested by my granddaughter, something suitable to their grade level. But, as I continued driving, I happened to think of Stanley, the poor orphan boy who wrote his autobiography in the hope that "the story of my efforts, struggles, suffering, and failures, of the work done, and the work left undone . . . can teach some lessons, and give encouragement to others." And by "others," he meant primarily unfortunates like himself who had endured or were enduring cruel childhoods. So, that day I did not read to the students the story of Ranger Rick and Ollie the Otter. Instead, I told them the story of Stanley. It moved them, I think. Through the magic of his words, his experience, I like to believe they came to identify with him. This short, simple episode confirmed, for me at least, that Stanley's life, Stanley's narrative, has power—one hundred years later.

What follows, let me be clear, is not the complete account of Stanley's life—just a portion, his "May of life," if you will. The story I have chosen to share opens in February 1859, with Stanley standing on the levee at New Orleans, age eighteen. He was not even named Stanley then; indeed, he had been baptized "John Rowlands, Bastard"—illegitimate son of a promiscuous barmaid and a man thought to have been John Rowlands, an "utter failure" who had died some years before of alcoholism, a man Stanley never knew.[1] His mother, for that matter, was indifferent to her firstborn, so Stanley was raised by a stern but responsible grandfather. But the grandfather died within a few years, and following his death Stanley's relatives decided, less than a month after the boy's sixth birthday, to save money and trouble by placing him in the workhouse. Although promised he was going to live with loving cousins, the child was betrayed and deposited at the front door of St. Asaph Union Workhouse, where he would remain until the age of fifteen and where he would manage somehow to receive a fair education.[2] Three years later, at age eighteen, after working as a tutor, farm laborer, haberdasher, and delivery boy, Stanley became a deckhand on the packet-ship *Windermere* bound for New Orleans. At sea, the young Welshman found himself abused once again, this time at the hands of a capricious captain and a brutal mate. But the "Welsh monkey" had learned well the art of survival at St. Asaph's, and fifty-two days after

    1. Henry Morton Stanley (HMS) was born January 28, 1841, in Denbigh, Wales. For a full discussion of his parentage and early childhood in Wales see Richard Hall, *Stanley: An Adventurer Explored* (Boston: Houghton Mifflin, 1975), 99–104.

    2. "At fifteen he was the height (5 feet, 5 inches) he would remain." Short, stocky, powerful, one could tell at a glance he was a moody, explosive loner who "lived within himself" (Frank J. McLynn, *Stanley: The Making of an African Explorer* [Chelsea, Mich.: Scarborough House, 1990], 85).

Henry Morton Stanley at age fifteen

setting sail from Liverpool he arrived in a promising new world. Without a thought, he jumped ship and danced on the dock.

Ghosts, however, pursued. They are present throughout the *Autobiography*, and, in his attempt to make sense of his past, Stanley reinvents himself, going to great lengths to reconstruct his boyhood. Unfortunately he conceals, he evades, he misleads. Frank J. McLynn, one of Stanley's three able modern biographers, goes so far as to declare the autobiography "largely a work of neurotic fantasy."[3] This is gross overstatement, I believe. Nevertheless, some of what follows is distorted, misleading, fabricated, particularly the chapter where Stanley discovers a father and mother and is transformed, à la Shaw's Doolittles. I considered omitting this chapter, "I Find a Father." To have done so, however, would have seriously damaged the narrative. An artificial editorial bridge would have been required, which would have altered the voice and flow of Stanley's story.

This relationship between Henry Morton Stanley and his "father" Henry Hope Stanley has fascinated biographers and researchers for al-

3. McLynn, *Stanley*, 29n.

most a century. Although carefully disguised in the *Autobiography*, it is believed that "some time around the end of 1859 or early 1860 a decisive rupture took place." Later in life the younger Stanley "refused to discuss the details, but they were said to involve a local girl with whom [he] had been too familiar," contends biographer Richard Hall. Stanley found his father's rejection to be too painful to admit, and his reaction, McLynn writes, "was of a piece with his treatment of earlier father-figures: he simply 'killed off' his protector."[4]

It is patently untrue that young Stanley traveled two years up and down the Mississippi with Henry Hope Stanley, then was sent to a friend's plantation in Arkansas when the elder Stanley set out for Cuba, where he supposedly died. Not only did the elder Stanley remain very much alive after 1861, but young Stanley is shown at Cypress Bend, Arkansas, in the household of Isaac Altshur in mid-August 1860.[5]

That Henry Hope Stanley befriended young John Rowlands, however, there is little doubt. Henry Hope Stanley was known in New Orleans for his kindness; "everyone liked him," reported a contemporary. Young Stanley, in the opinion of his biographers, probably proved unmanageable, or his father "began to find the lad's doglike adoration and demands for affection altogether more than he could comfortably handle."[6] Probably Stanley, as was his habit, ran away—more than once.

Throughout his life Henry Morton Stanley would leave a stream of broken associations and relationships in his wake. Perhaps the most painful for him, other than that with his mother, was this break with the Stanleys. He would spend the remainder of his life covering it with camouflage. The hurt must have been unbearable.

There are serious omissions within the *Autobiography*. With the help of information provided by Stanley's biographers, I will attempt to point out inaccuracies and distortions, and deceptions; but, even forewarned, the reader should approach the writings of this man so badly damaged by childhood with great caution. He can be vengeful with his

4. McLynn, *Stanley*, 37; Hall, *Stanley*, 123; McLynn, *Stanley*, 37. See also Jakob Wassermann, *Bula Matari: Stanley, Conqueror of a Continent* (New York: Liveright, 1933), 25; John Bierman, *Dark Safari: The Life Behind the Legend of Henry Morton Stanley* (New York: Alfred A. Knopf, 1990), 28.

5. From the 1860 Census of Arkansas County, Arkansas, HH 599, Douglas township, South Bend post office. Even "by his own account—the young Stanley arrived in Cypress Bend at least a year earlier, in January 1861" (Bierman, *Dark Safari*, 27–28).

6. Hall, *Stanley*, 122; Bierman, *Dark Safari*, 27.

pen and, at times, terribly wrongheaded. Were all this not bad enough, Stanley's manuscript was prepared for publication by his wife, Dorothy, after his death. Lady Stanley scrubbed and scissored, particularly the sections dealing with other women. Fortunately, the sections on Arkansas and the Confederate Army appear to have pretty well escaped fanciful reconstruction and bloody cleansing. They are solid. The account of Shiloh reveals that Stanley took great care to be accurate and even consulted the series of articles, written by participants, that appeared in *Century Magazine* from November 1884 to November 1887, as well as the *Official Records*.

As editor I have let Stanley's account stand as it appears in the portion of his autobiography beginning in 1859 and ending in 1865. I have made very few corrections of his often confusing and heavy-handed punctuation; obvious typographical errors I have set right, but when in doubt I left them alone. In the notes I have attempted to clarify, to identify, and to interpret. But this is Stanley's story, not the editor's. With respect to that, I have attempted to avoid crowding the pages for the sake of providing information easily obtained from one of Stanley's biographies.

Despite my admonition to be skeptical, I believe that the brooding Stanley provides a view of the American Civil War valuable and entertaining. What did he think of Confederate and Union soldiers? Of their causes? Of slavery? Of prewar plantation Arkansas? Of New Orleans? After all that this great Victorian had experienced, how did he look back as a man of fifty upon his youth in a new country? How did he view war itself? "I only record such incidents as affected me," Stanley explains, "and such as clearly stand out conspicuously in the retrospect, which have been not only a delight to memory, but which I am incapable of forgetting."

As the consummate man of action, a man legendary for his toughness, for his fierce stone visage and distant manner that made those near him uneasy, Stanley's narrative offers surprises. He writes, as may be expected, with energy, but also with tenderness, color, and charm. Sometimes he can't wait to leap ahead, switching excitedly from third person to first, then back to third. Supposedly this ruthless explorer had no sense of humor, but I found myself smiling here and there. As a product of a Victorian world, Stanley makes prudish pronouncements;

Dickensian lines, indeed scenes, jump out; and, as though high opera, the action will stop, allowing the narrator time to reflect, to moralize. No matter; within Stanley's story, his "short history," lives at once an observer and a participant, and, in my opinion, a man with depth of feeling—a hero, if you will—worthy of admiration.

1

At Sea

Though about thirty-five years have elapsed since I first stood upon the levee of the Crescent City, scarcely one of all my tumultuous sensations of pleasure, wonder, and curiosity, has been forgotten by me. The levee sloped down with a noble breadth to the river, and stretched for miles up and down in front of the city, and was crowded with the cargoes of the hundreds of vessels which lay broadside to it. In some places the freights lay in mountainous heaps, but the barrels, and hogsheads, and cotton bales, covered immense spaces, though arranged in precise order; and, with the multitudes of men,—white, red, black, yellow,— horses, mules, and drays and wagons, the effect of such a scene, with its fierce activity and new atmosphere, upon a raw boy from St. Asaph,[1] may be better imagined than described.

During my fifty-two days of ship-life there had filtered into my mind curious ideas respecting the new land of America and the character of the people.[2] In a large measure they were more complimentary than otherwise; but the levee of New Orleans carried with its name a reputation for slung-shots, doctored liquor, Shanghai-ing, and wharf-ratting,

1. St. Asaph Union Workhouse, where HMS lived from 1847 to 1856. A Commission of Inquiry found it to be a "nursery of female prostitution and male obscenity" (McLynn, *Stanley*, 18. See also Ian Anstruther, *Dr. Livingston, I Presume?* [New York: E. P. Dutton, 1957], 10–11; Hall, *Stanley*, 104–108).

2. For his account of sailing from Liverpool to New Orleans see Stanley, *The Autobiography of Sir Henry Morton Stanley*, ed. Dorothy T. Stanley (New York: Houghton Mifflin, 1909), 69–81.

which made it a dubious place for me. When Harry[3] directed my attention to the numerous liquor saloons fronting the river-side, all the scandalous stories I had heard of knifing, fighting, and manslaughter, recurred at once to my mind, and made me very shy of these haunts of villainy and deviltry. As he could not forego the pleasure of introducing me to a city which he had constantly praised, he insisted that I should accompany him for a walk that first night up Tchoupitoulas Street, and to some "diggins" where he had acquaintances. I accepted his invitation without any misgiving, or any other thought than of satisfying a natural curiosity.

I think it is one of the most vivid recollections I possess. The details of my first impressions, and an analysis of my thoughts, would fill many pages. Of the thousands of British boys who have landed in this city, I fancy none was so utterly unsophisticated as myself—for reasons which have already been related.

Directly the sun was set, we were relieved from duty, and were allowed liberty to go ashore. We flew over the planking laid across the ships, light as young fawns; and, when I felt the shore under my feet, I had to relieve myself by an ecstatic whirl or two about Harry, crying out, "At last! At last! New Orleans! It is too good to be true!" I was nearly overwhelmed with blissful feeling that rises from emancipation. I was free!—and I was happy, yes, actually happy, for I was free—at last the boy was free!

We raced across the levee, for joy begets activity, and activity is infectious. What was a vivid joy to me, was the delight of gratified pride to Harry. "I told you," he said, beaming, "what New Orleans was. Is it not grand?" But "grand" did not convey its character, as it appeared to my fresh young eyes. Some other word was wanted to express the whole of what I felt. The soft, balmy air, with its strange scents of fermenting molasses, semi-baked sugar, green coffee, pitch, Stockholm tar, brine of mess-beef, rum, and whiskey drippings contributed a great deal towards imparting the charm of romance to everything I saw. The people I passed appeared to me to be nobler than any I had seen. They had a swing of the body wholly un-English, and their facial expressions differed from those I had been accustomed to. I strove hard to give a name

3. A young English shipmate aboard the *Windermere* who had made the voyage to New Orleans previously.

to what was so unusual. Now, of course, I know that it was the sense of equality and independence that made each face so different from what I had seen in Liverpool. These people knew no master, and had no more awe of their employers than they had of their fellow-employees.

We reached the top of Tchoupitoulas Street, the main commercial artery of the city. The people were thronging home from the business quarters, to the more residential part. They passed by in many hundreds, with their lunch-buckets, and, though soiled by their labours, they were not wearied or depressed. In the vicinity of Poydras Street, we halted before a boarding-house, where Harry was welcomed with the warmth which is the due of the returned voyager. He ordered dinner, and, with appetites sharpened by youth and ocean airs, we sat down to a spread of viands which were as excellent as they were novel. Okra soup, grits, sweet potatoes, brinjalls,[4] corn pones, mush-pudding, and "fixings"—every article but the bread was strange and toothsome. Harry appropriated my praise of the meal to himself, paid for it with the air of one whose purse was deep beyond soundings, and then invested a silver piece in cigars; for American boys always smoked cigars, and, when in New Orleans, English boys loved to imitate them.[5]

Now, when I stepped on the levee, frisky as a lamb, I was about as good as a religious observance of the Commandments can make one. To me those were the principal boundary-stones that separated the region of right from that of wrong. Between the greater landmarks, there were many well-known minor indexes; but there were some which were almost undiscoverable to one so young and untravelled as I was. Only the angelically-immaculate could tread along the limits of right and wrong without a misstep.

After dinner we sauntered through a few streets, in a state of sweet content, and, by and by, entered another house, the proprietress of which was extremely gracious. Harry whispered something to her, and we were shown to a room called a parlour. Presently, there bounced in four gay young ladies, in such scant clothing that I was speechless with amazement. My ignorance of their profession was profound, and I was willing enough to be enlightened; but, when they proceeded to take liberties with my person, they seemed to me to be so appallingly wicked

4. Fruit of the eggplant.
5. For HMS in New Orleans see Hall, *Stanley*, 118–20; McLynn, *Stanley*, 33–37.

that I shook them off and fled out of the house. Harry followed me, and, with all the arts he could use, tried to induce me to return; but I would as soon have jumped into the gruel-coloured Mississippi as have looked into the eyes of those giggling wantons again. My disgust was so great that I never, in after years, could overcome my repugnance to females of that character.

Then Harry persuaded me to enter a bar-room, and called for liquor, but here, again, I was obstinate. "Drink yourself, if you like," said I, "but I belong to the Band of Hope and have signed the pledge, so I must not."[6]

"Well smoke then, do something like other fellows," he said, offering me my choice.

As I had never heard that smoking was a moral offence, and had a desire to appear manly, I weakly yielded, and, putting a great cigar between my lips, puffed proudly and with vigour. But alas! my punishment was swift. My head seemed to swim, and my limbs were seized with a trembling; and, while vainly trying to control myself, a surge of nausea quite overpowered me, and I tried to steal back to the ship, as abjectly contrite as ever repentant wretch could well be.[7] Thus ended my first night at New Orleans.

Harry's story of the two English boys, who had been compelled to abscond from the *Windermere*[8] the voyage before, recurred to me more than once after Nelson's greeting next morning. "Hello! you here still! I thought you had vamoosed like the Irish stowaways. Not enough physic, eh? Well, sonny, we must see what we can do for you."[9]

I was put to cleaning brass-work—a mechanical occupation that breeds thought. If, attracted by a lively levee scene, I lifted my eyes, one

6. The Band of Hope was a British temperance society for working-class children organized in Leeds in 1847. Children might enroll at age six if they would take a vow of total abstinence.

7. Despite his ordeal, HMS would remain faithful to his "Havanas" for the rest of his life (Lucy M. Jones and Ivor Wynne, *H. M. Stanley and Wales* [St. Asaph: H. M. Stanley Exhibition Committee, 1972], 21).

8. "Lloyd's records show that the *Windermere* was a ship rig, 1,107 tons, registered at the port of Boston, the master David Hardinge, and that she had sailed from Liverpool five days before Christmas 1858" (Anstruther, *Dr. Livingstone, I Presume?* 18).

9. Nelson, the bullying second mate of the *Windermere* (see Bierman, *Dark Safari*, 15, 20).

Stanley at age seventeen

or other of the mates bawled out, "Now, you scalawag, or, you little
sweep, what in _____ are you doing? Get on with that work, you
putty-faced son of a _____!" and so on! Ever some roaring blasphemy, some hideous epithet, with a kick or a clout, until, on the fifth
day, conviction stole upon every sense that it was to a set purpose; and
my small remnant of self-respect kindled into a revolt. I understand
now that it was the pitiful sum of money due to me they wished to save
for the ship-owners or captain, that prevented them from saying right
out, "You may go, and be _____ to you." Such a dismissal entailed a

settlement.[10] Just as Moses Owen[11] lacked the moral courage to despatch me from his presence, these men were at the same game of nagging; and it succeeded in inspiring indifference as to what would become of me. I could say, at last, "Better to rot on this foreign strand than endure this slave's life longer."[12]

That evening I declined to go ashore with Harry, and sat pondering in the loneliness of my cabin, and prayer, somewhat fallen into disuse of late, was remembered; and I rose from my knees primed for the venture. Habit of association, as usual with me, had knit some bonds of attachment between me and the ship. She connected me with England; by her I came, and by her I could return. Now that was impossible; I must follow the stowaways, and leave the floating hell for ever.

I lit the swinging pewter lamp, emptied my sea-bag on the floor, and out of its contents picked my best shore clothes, and the bishop's Bible. I dressed myself with care, and, blowing out the lamp, lay down. By and by, Harry reeled in, half-stupefied with his excesses, rolled into his bunk above me; and, when he was unconscious, I rose and glided out. Five minutes later, I was hurrying rapidly along the river-side of the levee; and, when about half a mile from the ship, I plunged into the shadows caused by a pile of cotton bales, and lay down to await day-break.

10. "Now at last he realised why Captain Hardinge had been so ready to sign him on. Hardinge and his officers ran a racket which involved pocketing the wages of their deckhands. Their method was simple. They made their young charges' lives such hell on board that the boys would jump ship at the first port rather than endure further brutality" (McLynn, *Stanley*, 32).

11. HMS's cousin, the school head at Brynford, who grew to resent HMS because he "sensed Stanley's intellectual distinction" and feared he "might soon outstrip his own intellectual attainments" (McLynn, *Stanley*, 25. See also Stanley, *Autobiography*, 49–51; Hall, *Stanley*, 99–112).

12. This quotation has not been identified, but a somewhat similar phrase is attributed to Ellen Craft, a former slave: "I had much rather starve in England a free woman than to be a slave for the best man that ever breathed upon the continent" (Richard Newman, ed., *African-American Quotations* [Phoenix: Oryx Press, 1998], 324).

2

At Work

Soon after sunrise I came out of my nest, and after dusting myself, strode towards Tchoupitoulas Street.

> "The world was all before me where to choose,
> And Providence my guide."[1]

The absolutely penniless has a choice of two things, work or starve. No boy of my age and vitality could deliberately choose starvation. The other alternative remained to me, and for work, work of any kind, I was most ready; with a strong belief that it was the only way to achieve that beautiful independence which sat so well on those who had succeeded. I was quite of the opinion of my Aunt Mary, that "rolling stones gathered no moss," and I wanted permanent work, wherein I could approve myself steady, and zealously industrious.[2] Hitherto, I had been most un-

1. HMS is attempting to quote Milton, *Paradise Lost*, book 12, line 646: "The world was all before them, where to choose / Their place of rest, and Providence their guide."
2. Mary Owen, the eldest sister of HMS's mother, Elizabeth Parry, lived close to the Bynford school run by her twenty-three-year-old son Moses. There with the help of her youngest son, David, Owen "combined small-scale farming with shopkeeping" on a place called Ffynnon Beuno. After being discharged from St. Asaph's in 1856 at age fifteen, HMS would enter this school run by his cousin and serve as a monitor (pupil-teacher). His aunt, according to McLynn, opposed HMS's enrollment, believing it would prove detrimental financially to her son. Nevertheless, she allowed HMS to earn enough money working on her farm to pay for a proper set of clothes. Following nine months at the school, HMS found himself at cross-purposes with his cousin, and he returned to Ffynnon Beuno only to be viewed by his aunt as the "the fruit of [her sister's] sinfulness." HMS, however, would remain and work as a laborer on her farm for more than a year,

fortunate in the search. Respectful civility, prompt obedience, and painstaking zeal, had been at a discount; but, such is the buoyancy of healthy youth, I still retained my faith that decent employment was within reach of the diligent, and it was this that I was now bent upon.

Hastening across the levee, I entered the great commercial street of the city, at a point not far from St. Thomas Street, and, after a little inward debate, continued down Tchoupitoulas Street, along the sidewalk, with all my senses wide-awake. I read every sign reflectively. The store-owners' names were mostly foreign, and suggestive of Teutonic and Hibernian origin; but the larger buildings were of undeniable Anglo-Saxon. At the outset, lager-beer saloons were frequent; then followed more shanties, with rusty tin roofs; but, beyond these, the stores were more massive and uniform, and over the doors were the inscriptions, "Produce and Commission Merchants," etc.

As I proceeded, looking keenly about for the favourable chance, the doors were flung open one by one, and I obtained a view of the interior. Negroes commenced to sweep the long alleys between the goods piles, and to propel the dust and rubbish of the previous day's traffic towards the open gutter. Then flour, whiskey, and rum barrels, marked and branded, were rolled out, and arranged near the kerbstone. Hogsheads and tierces were set on end, cases were built up, sacks were laid in orderly layers, awaiting removal by the drays, which, at a later hour, would convey them to the river-steamers.

Soon after seven, I had arrived near the end of the long street; and I could see the colossal Custom-House, and its immense scaffolding.[3] So far, I had not addressed myself to a single soul, and I was thinking I should have to search in another street; when, just at this time, I saw a gentleman of middle age seated in front of No. 3 store, reading a morning newspaper. From his sober dark alpaca suit and tall hat, I took him

---

and he would quote his aunt Mary for the rest of his life—usually her sayings about frugality and the stern demands of a virtuous life (McLynn, *Stanley*, 23–26; Anstruther, *Dr. Livingstone, I Presume?* 8–9, 15).

3. The Custom House was enormous, one of the largest buildings in the United States at that time. When HMS was in New Orleans, Col. Pierre G. T. Beauregard would have been the superintendent of construction. Work had begun on the structure in 1848, and it was not completed until 1881 (Arthur J. Scully, *James Dakin, Architect: His Career in New York and the South* [Baton Rouge: Louisiana State University Press, 1973], 162–84. See also Mary Louise Christovich, Roulhac Toledano, Betty Swanson, and Pat Holder, *New Orleans Architecture*, vol. 1 [Gretna, La.: Pelican Publishing, 1972], 1:131).

to be the proprietor of the building, over the door of which was the sign, "Speake and McCreary, Wholesale and Commission Merchants." He sat tilted back against what appeared to be the solid granite frame of the door, with a leisured ease which was a contrast to the activity I had previously noticed. After a second look at the respectable figure and genial face, I ventured to ask,—

"Do you want a boy, sir?"

"Eh?" he demanded with a start; "what did you say?"

"I want some work, sir; I asked if you wanted a boy."

"A boy," he replied slowly, and fixedly regarding me. "No, I do not think I want one. What should I want a boy for? Where do you hail from? You are not an American."[4]

"I came from Liverpool, sir, less than a week ago, by a packet-ship. I shipped as cabin-boy; but, when we got to sea, I was sent forward, and, until last night, I was abused the whole voyage. At last, I became convinced that I was not wanted, and left. As you are the first gentleman I have seen, I thought I would apply to you for work, or ask you for advice how to get it."

"So," he ejaculated, tilting his chair back again. "You are friendless in a strange land, eh, and want work to begin making your fortune, eh? Well, what work can you do? Can you read? What book is that in your pocket?"

"It is my Bible, a present from our Bishop. Oh, yes, sir, I can read," I replied proudly.

He held out his hand and said, "Let me see your Bible."

He opened it at the fly-leaves, and smiled, as he read the inscription, "Presented to John Rowlands by the Right Revd. Thomas Vowler Short, D.D., Lord Bishop of St. Asaph, for diligent application to his studies, and general good conduct. January 5th, 1855."[5]

Returning it to me, he pointed to an article in his newspaper, and said, "Read that." It was something about a legislative assembly, which I delivered, as he said, "very correctly, but with an un-American accent."

4. Henry Hope Stanley (HHS) was a native of Cheshire close to the section of Wales where HMS was raised. Thus he "could not have failed to recognize the boy's Welsh accent" (Bierman, *Dark Safari*, 26).

5. See Cadwalader Rowlands, *H. M. Stanley: The Story of His Life* (London: n.p., 1872), 5.

"Can you write well?" he next asked.

"Yes, sir, a good round-hand, as I have been told."

"Then let me see you mark that coffee-sack, with the same address you see on the one near it. There is the marking pot and brush."

In a few seconds, I had traced "⟨S⟩ MEMPHIS, TENN.," and looked up.

"Neatly done," he said; "now proceed and mark the other sacks in the same way."

There were about twenty of them, and in a few minutes they were all addressed.

"Excellent," he cried; "even better than I could do it myself. There is no chance of my coffee getting lost *this* time! Well, I must see what can be done for you. Dan," he cried to a darkie indoors, "when is Mr. Speake likely to be in?"

"Bout nine, sah, mebbe a leetle aftah."

"Oh, well," said he, looking at his watch, "we have ample time before us. As I don't suppose you have breakfasted yet, you had better come along with me. Take the paper, Dan."

We turned down the next street, and as we went along he said first impressions were very important in this world, and he feared that if his friend James Speake[6] had seen cotton fluff and dust on my jacket, and my uncombed hair, he might not be tempted to look at me twice, or care to trust me among his groceries; but, after a breakfast, a hair-cut, and a good clean-up, he thought I would have a better chance of being employed.

I was taken to a restaurant, where I was provided with superb coffee, sugared waffles, and doughnuts, after which we adjourned to a basement distinguished by a pole with red, white, and blue paint.

Everyone who has been operated upon by an American barber will understand the delight I felt, as I lay submissive in the luxurious chair, to be beautified by a demi-semi-gentleman with ambrosial curls! The mere fact that such as he condescended to practise his art upon one who but yesterday was only thought worthy of a kick, gave an increased value to my person, and provoked my conceit. When my dark hair had

6. James Speake was co-owner of the grocery Speake & McCreary, 3 Tchoupitoulas Street (Charles Gardner, *Gardner's New Orleans Directory for the Year 1859* [New Orleans: C. Gardner, 1858], 278).

been artistically shortened, my head and neck shampooed, and my face glowed with the scouring, I looked into the mirror and my vanity was prodigious. A negro boy completed my toilet with an efficient brushing and a boot-polish, and my friend was pleased to say that I looked first-rate.[7]

By the time we returned to Speake and McCreary's store, Mr. James Speake had put in an appearance. After a cordial greeting, my benefactor led Mr. Speake away by the arm and held a few minutes' earnest conversation with him. Presently I was beckoned to advance, and Mr. Speake said with a smile to me,—

"Well, young man, this gentleman tells me you want a place. Is that so?"

"Yes, sir."

"That is all right. I am willing to give you a week's trial at five dollars, and if we then find we suit each other, the place will be permanent. Are you agreeable?"

There could be no doubt of that fact, and Mr. Speake turned round to two young gentlemen, one of whom he called Mr. Kennicy, and the other Mr. Richardson,[8] and acquainted them with my engagement as a help to Mr. Richardson in the shipping business. The generosity of my unknown friend had been so great that, before addressing myself to any employment, I endeavoured to express my gratitude; but my strong emotions were not favourable to spontaneous fluency. The gentleman seemed to divine what I wished to say, and said,—

"There, that will do. I know what is in your heart. Shake hands. I am going up-river with my consignments, but I shall return shortly and hope to hear the best accounts of you."

For the first half-hour my heart was too full, and my eyes too much blurred, to be particularly bright. The gentleman's benevolence had been immense, and as yet I knew not even his name, his business, or what connection he had with the store of Speake and McCreary. I was in the midst of strangers, and, so far, my experience of them had not been of that quality to inspire confidence. In a short time, however, Mr.

7. McLynn believes HMS had a preoccupation with clothes and neatness generally, to the point of neurosis, "an obsessive tidiness, which first manifested itself in the months at the Speake store" (McLynn, *Stanley*, 36).

8. Probably W. F. Richardson, a clerk employed at 182 Tchoupitoulas Street in 1858 (Gardner, *New Orleans Directory*, 252).

Richardson's frankness and geniality made me more cheerful. He appeared to take pride in inducting me into my duties, and I responded with alacrity. He had an extremely pleasant manner, the candour of Harry, without his vulgarity. Before an hour had passed, I was looking up to him as to a big brother, and was asking him all sorts of questions respecting the gentleman who had taken me out of the street and started me so pleasantly in life.

From Mr. Richardson I learned that he [Henry Hope Stanley] was a kind of broker who dealt between planters up-river and merchants in New Orleans, and traded through a brother with Havana and other West Indian ports.[9] He had a desk in the store, which he made use of when in town, and did a good deal of safe business in produce both with Mr. Speake and other wholesale merchants.[10] He travelled much up and down the river, taking large consignments with him for back settlements up the Arkansas, Washita, and Saline, and other rivers, and returning often with cotton and other articles. *His name was MR. STANLEY.* His wife lived in St. Charles Street, in a first-class boarding-house, and, from the style Mr. and Mrs. Stanley kept up, he thought they must be pretty well off.[11] This was the extent of the information

9. HHS was born in England in 1811 and emigrated to Charleston in 1836. He left South Carolina and moved to Texas where he married. The young couple established their home in New Orleans where Mrs. Stanley died of yellow fever in 1843. He remarried in 1846 to Miss Frances Meller, a fifteen-year-old woman also English born. In the Stanleys' home on Annunciation Square lived two girls whom the couple had adopted but whom HMS fails to mention. HHS became wealthy in New Orleans as a cotton factor and as "the senior member of a partnership which owned two large cotton presses" (Bierman, *Dark Safari*, 26–27. For background on HHS, see Catherine M. Dillon, "From Wharf Waif to Knighthood," *Roosevelt Review* 7 [June 1944]: 23, 27–33; John S. Kendall, "Old New Orleans Houses and Some of the People Who Lived in Them," *Louisiana Historical Quarterly* 20 [July–September 1937]: 815–16; McLynn, *Stanley*, 35; Mary Willis Shuey, "Stanley in New Orleans," *Southwest Review* 25 [1939–40]: 378–93).

10. HHS owned the Mississippi Cotton Press, "long a conspicuous feature in Tchoupitoulas Street," and it was there HMS would clerk (Kendall, "Old New Orleans Houses," 816–17. See also Federal Writers Project, New Orleans, *New Orleans City Guide.* [Boston: Houghton Mifflin, 1938], 347).

11. According to the New Orleans City Directory for 1859, the Stanleys' home was located at 904 Orange Street on Annunciation Square. Indeed, "scratched on one of the window panes in a small rear room of the house is the name 'Stanley,' resembling the signature of the famous explorer," reveals a 1938 New Orleans guidebook. HHS was also the owner of a "huge plantation called Jefferson Hall in Tangipa Hoa [sic] parish near Arcola," according to McLynn (Gardner, *New Orleans Directory*, 279; New Orleans Fed-

Mr. Richardson could give me, which was most gratifying, and assured me that I had at least one friend in the strange city.

There have been several memorable occasions in my life; but, among them, this first initial stage towards dignity and independence must ever be prominent. What a proud, glad holiday-spirit moved me then! I soon became sensible of a kindling elation of feeling, for the speech of all to me was as though everyone recognised that I had entered into the great human fraternity. The abruptness of the transition, from the slave of yesterday into the free-man of to-day, endowed with a sacred inviolability of person, astonished me. Only a few hours ago, I was as one whose skull might be smashed at the impulse of a moment; and now, in an instant, as it were, I was free of the severe thraldom, and elevated to the rank of man.

Messrs. Kennicy and Richardson were good types of free-spoken young America. They were both touchy in the extreme, and, on points of personal honour, highly intolerant. America breeds such people by thousands, who appear to live eternally on the edge of resentment, and to be as inflammable as tinder. It is dangerous to deal with them in badinage, irony, sarcasm, or what we call "chaff." Before the expiration of the first day, I had noted that their high spirits scarcely brooked a reproof, or contradiction, the slightest approach to anything of the kind exciting them to a strange heat. When I saw that they became undisguisedly angry because Mr. Speake happened to ask them why some order for goods had not been completed, I really could not help feeling a little contempt for them. Otherwise, they were both estimable young men, clean as new pins, exquisitely dressed, and eminently cordial— especially Richardson, whom I warmly admired.

My first day's employment consisted in assisting Dan and Samuel, the two negroes, in taking groceries on trucks from the depths of the long store to the sidewalk, or rolling liquor or flour-barrels on the edges of thin boards,—an art I acquired very soon,—and in marking sundry lots for shipment to Mississippi ports with strange names, such as Bayou Placquemine, Attakapas, Opelousas, etc., etc. Richardson was, in the meantime, busy in making out bills of lading, and arranging with the pursers of the steamers for their transportation. The drays clattered

---

eral Writers Project, *New Orleans City Guide*, 347; McLynn, *Stanley*, 35. See also Dillon, "From Wharf Waif to Knighthood," 29).

to the door, and removed the goods as fast as we could get them ready. Every moment of the day added to my rapture. The three lofts above the ground-floor contained piles upon piles of articles such as could be comprised under the term groceries, besides rare wines and brandies, liqueurs and syrups. The ground-floor was piled up to the ceiling almost with sacks of coffee-berries, grains, and cases of miscellanea, barrels of flour, tierces of bacon, hams, etc., etc. It was informing even to read the titles on the neatly-branded cases, which contained bottled fruit, tinned jams, berries of all kinds, scented soaps, candles, vermicelli, macaroni, and other strange things. If I but stepped on the sidewalk, I saw something new and unheard-of before. The endless drays thundering by the door, and the multitudes of human beings, not one of whom was like the other in head-gear or dress, had a fascination for me; and, with every sound and sight, I was learning something new.

While influenced by all these things, I sprang upon work of any kind with an avid desire to have it completed; but the negroes did their utmost to suppress my boisterous exuberance of spirit by saying, "Take it easy, little boss, don't kill yourself. Plenty of time. Leave something for to-morrow." Had the mates of the *Windermere* but looked in upon us, they might have learned that a happy crew had more work in them, than when driven by belaying-pins and rope's ends.

Towards evening we swept up; and, when we had tidied the store, it came to my mind that I knew no lodging-house. In consulting with Dan, he said he knew a Mrs. Williams, who kept a nice, cheap boarding-house on St. Thomas Street, where I could be most comfortable. It was arranged that he should introduce me, and I walked up Tchoupitoulas Street, with the two slaves, whose tin lunch-buckets swung heavily, I thought, as they moved homeward.

Mrs. Williams, a young and black beauty, with intelligent features, was most affable, and agreed to board me at a rate which would leave me a respectable margin at the end of the week, and to give me a large attic room for myself.[12] Her house was of wood, with a garden in front, and a spacious tree-shaded yard at the rear. The maternal solicitude she showed in providing for my comfort greatly charmed me, though I was

12. The 1860 census, "while listing no John Rowlands, does name one 'J. Rolling,' described as a clerk born in England, as a boarder, with a number of other clerks and cotton brokers, at a house in St. Thomas Street" (Bierman, *Dark Safari*, 27).

forced to smile at her peculiar English and drawling accent. But when, just as I was about to retire to my bedroom, she, in the most matter-of-fact way, assisted me to undress, and took possession of my shirt and collar, saying they would be washed and ironed by morning, that I might look more "spruce," my estimation of her rose very high indeed, and affected me to such a degree that I revolved all the kindnesses I had experienced during the day, and was reminded to give thanks to Him, Who, "like as a father, pitieth his children and them that fear Him."

The next morning, by half-past six, I was at the door of Speake and McCreary's store, fit for any amount of work, and glorying in my condition. By eight o'clock the store, which was about one hundred feet long, was sweet and clean, the sidewalk was swept, and the earlier installments of goods duly arranged on it for shipment. Then the book-keeper and shipping-clerk entered, fresh and scented as for courtship, took off their street coats, and donning their linen "dusters," resumed business. About nine, Mr. James Speake—McCreary was dead—appeared with the mien of gracious masterhood, which to me was a sign of goodness, and stimulative of noble efforts in his service.[13]

My activity and fresh memory were soon appreciated. Half-a-dozen times a day my ready answers saved time. My hearing seemed to them to be phenomenal; and my accuracy in remembering the numbers of kegs, cases, and sacks remaining in store, caused me, before the end of the week, to be as a kind of walking inventory. I could tell where each article was located, and the contents of the various lofts had also been committed to my memory. Unlike the young gentlemen, I never argued, or contradicted, or took advantage of a pettish ebullition to aggravate temper; and, what was a great relief to persons with responsibilities in a warm climate, I was always at hand, near the glass-

13. Dorothy Tennant Stanley (DTS) writes: "Early in 1891, I visited New Orleans, with my husband. He tried to find the houses and places he had known as a boy. The following remarks are from his notebook—'We walked up Canal Street, and took the cars at Tchoupitoulas Street, as far as Annunciation Street. Looked at No. 1659, which resembles the house I sought; continued down to No.1323—above Thalis Street; this also resembled the house, but it is now occupied by two families; in former days, the house had but one occupant. I seemed to recognize it by its attics. The houses no doubt have been renumbered. We then returned to Tchoupitoulas Street, and thence into St. Peter's Street, which formerly was, I think, Commerce Street. Speake's house was between Common and Canal Street—No. 3. Here, also, there has been a change; No. 3 is now No. 5. The numbers of the next houses are now in the hundreds' " (Stanley, *Autobiography*, 93n).

door of the office, awaiting orders. Previous to my arrival, Dan and Samuel had always found something to do at a distance, either upstairs or in the back-yard; they pretended not to hear; and it had been a fatiguing task to call them, and trying to the patience to wait for them; but now I was within easy hail, and my promptitude was commended. Thereupon my week's trial ended satisfactorily, even more so than I had anticipated, for I was permanently engaged at twenty-five dollars a month. Such a sum left me with fifteen dollars a month, net, after payment of board and lodging, and was quite a fortune in my eyes. Mr. Speake, moreover, advanced a month's pay, that I might procure an outfit. Mr. Richardson, who boarded in the more fashionable Rampart Street, undertook to assist in my purchases, and presented me with a grand, brass-bound trunk of his own, which, besides having a tray for shirts, and a partition for neck-ties and collars, was adorned on the lid with the picture of a lovely maiden. Truly, a boy is easily pleased! I had more joy in contemplating that first trunk of mine, and imprisoning my treasures under lock and key, than I have had in any property since!

My rating was now a junior clerk. Our next-door neighbours, Messrs. Hall and Kemp, employed two junior clerks, whose pay was four hundred dollars a year.[14] They were happy, careless lads, who dressed well, and whose hardest toil was with the marking-pot. I was now as presentable as they, but I own to be proud that I had no fear of soiling my hands or clothes with work, and I never allowed a leaky sack of coffee, or barrel of flour, to leave our store for want of a little sewing or coopering—tasks which they felt it to be beneath them to do!

Long before the *Windermere* had sailed back for Liverpool with her cotton cargo, a great change had come over me. Up to my arrival in New Orleans, no indulgence had been shown me. I was scarcely an hour away from the supervision of someone. From my nurse's maternal care, I had passed under the strict régime of the Orphan's Academy—the Workhouse [St. Asaph's]; thence I had been transferred to the no-less-strict guardianship of Aunt Mary, and the severe Moses, thence into that of Uncle Tom;[15] and, afterwards, had tasted of the terrible dis-

14. The firm of Hall, Kemp & Co. (John Kemp, Sr., John Kemp, Jr., and John M. Hall) was located at 1 Tchoupitoulas Street (Gardner, *New Orleans Directory*, 124, 167).
15. Thomas Morris had married HMS's aunt Maria Parry. Morris believed he could find HMS employment in Liverpool as a clerk and invited the boy to live with them. Full of hope, HMS left Ffynnon Beuno and went to Liverpool. Disaster followed. The job

cipline of an American packet-ship [*Windermere*]. Draconian rules had been prescribed; the birch hung ever in view in one place, censure and menace at another. At Uncle Tom's there was no alternative but obedience or the street; and the packet-ship was furnished with rope's ends and belaying-pins. But, within a few weeks of arriving in America, I had become different in temper and spirit. That which was natural in me, though so long repressed, had sprung out very quickly under the peculiar influence of my surroundings. The childish fear of authority had fled—for authority no longer wore its stern, relentless aspect, but was sweetly reasonable. Those who exercised it were gentle and sociable, and I repaid them with respect and gratitude. To them I owed my happiness; and my new feeling of dignity made me stretch myself to my full height, and revel luxuriously in fond ideas. I possessed properties in my person which I instinctively valued, and felt bound to cultivate. The two-feet square of the street I occupied were mine for the time being, and no living man could budge me except at his peril. The view of the sky was as freely mine as another's. These American rights did not depend on depth of pocket, or stature of a man, but every baby had as much claim to them as the proudest merchant. Neither poverty nor youth was degrading, nor was it liable to abuse from wealth or age. Besides my youth, activity, and intelligence, of which I had been taught the value, I had become conscious of the fact that I possessed privileges of free speech, free opinions, immunity from insult, oppression, and the contempt of class; and that, throughout America, my treatment from men would solely depend upon my individual character, without regard of family or pedigree. These were proud thoughts. I respired more freely, my shoulders rose considerably, my back straightened, my strides became longer, as my mind comprehended this new feeling of independence. To the extent of so much I could not be indebted to any man living; but for the respectability of the covering and comfort of the body, and the extension of my rights to more ground than I could occupy standing, I must work.

Inspired of these thoughts, I was becoming as un-English in disposition as though I had been forty years in the land, and, as old Sir Thomas

---

never materialized, and HMS presently found himself searching for any type of work and alienated from his uncle (Jones and Wynne, *H. M. Stanley and Wales*, 21; McLynn, *Stanley*, 26–28).

Browne puts it, "of a constitution so general that it consorted and sympathised" with things American.[16] My British antipathies and proclivit-
ies were dropping from me as rapidly as the littlenesses of my servile
life were replaced by the felicities of freedom. I shared in the citizens'
pride in their splendid port, the length and stability of their levee, their
unparalleled lines of shipping, their magnificent array of steamers, and
their majestic river. I believed, with them, that their Custom-House,
when completed, would be a matchless edifice, that Canal Street was
unequalled for its breadth, that Tchoupitoulas Street was, beyond com-
pare, the busiest street in the world, that no markets equalled those of
New Orleans for their variety of produce, and that no city, not even
Liverpool, could exhibit such mercantile enterprise, or such a smart go-
ahead spirit, as old and young manifested in the chief city of the South.
I am not sure that I have lost all that lively admiration yet, though I
have since seen dozens of cities more populous, more cultivated, and
more opulent. Many years of travel have not extinguished my early
faith, but it would require ages to eradicate my affection for the city
which first taught me that a boy may become a *man*.

Had the joylessness of boyhood endured a few years longer, it is
probable that the power of joyousness would have dried up; but, fortunately, though I had seen fifteen summers, I was a mere child in experience. It was only eighteen months since I had left St. Asaph, and but
two months and a half since I had entered the world outside my family.
Since I became a man, I have often wondered what would have become
of me had my melting mood that last night at Roscommon Street lasted
a little longer. It was the turning-point of my life, I am disposed to
think, and it was good for me to have had the courage to say "No," at
that critical moment. A trifle more perseverance, on the part of Uncle
Tom, would have overcome my inclination for departure from England,
and made me a fixture within his own class.[17] On that occasion my

16. Sir Thomas Browne, *Religio Medici* (1643), part 2.

17. HMS seems to contradict himself. Earlier he had complained that his uncle Tom
and aunt Maria "were invariably partial to their own, when called to arbitrate between
us." Thus protected by his parents, cousin Teddy made HMS's life miserable. Money was
scarce in the household, and suitable employment for HMS could not be obtained, even
on the Liverpool docks. Presently HMS found himself adrift, "in a fair way of being
ground very fine." A chance errand took him aboard the *Windermere*, which was soon to
sail. The captain asked HMS if he would like to be the cabin boy, and he accepted on the
spot (Stanley, *Autobiography*, 66–68).

weakly, half-hearted negative served me to good purpose; but I should have been spared many trials had I been educated to utter my "Noes" more often, more loudly, and more firmly than I have; and I suppose most men have had cause to condemn that unsatisfactory education which sent them into the world so imperfectly equipped for moral resistance. In my opinion, the courage to deliver a proper "No" ought to be cultivated as soon as a child's intelligence is sufficiently advanced. The few times I have been able to say it have been productive of immense benefit to me, though to my shame, be it said, I yearned to say "Yes."

That soft habit of becoming fondly attached to associations, which made me weep on leaving St. Asaph, Ffynnon Beuno, Brynford, Liverpool, and even the *Windermere*, made me cling to my attic room in the house of Mrs. Williams. My increase of pay enabled me to secure a larger and more comfortable room; but, detesting change, I remained its occupant. My self-denial was compensated, however, by a fine surplus of dollars, with which I satisfied a growing desire for books.

So far, all the story-books I had read, beyond the fragments found in School-readers, consisted of that thrilling romance about Enoch and his brothers, a novelette called "First Footsteps in Evil," "Kaloolah," by Dr. Mayo, which I had found at Ffynnon Beuno, and "Ivanhoe," in three volumes, at which I had furtively glanced as it lay open in my cousin's study at Brynford.

Through the influence of cheap copies of standard books, millions of readers in America have been educated, at slight cost, in the best productions of English authors; and when these have been relegated to the second-hand bookstalls, it is wonderful what a library one can possess at a trifling expense. There was such a stall existing conveniently near St. Thomas Street, which I daily passed; and I could never resist fingering the books, and snatching brief delights from their pages. As soon as my wardrobe was established, I invested my surplus in purchases of this description, and the bookseller, seeing a promising customer in me, allowed me some latitude in my selection, and even catered to my tastes. The state of the binding mattered little; it was the contents that fascinated me. My first prize that I took home was Gibbon's "Decline and Fall," in four volumes, because it was associated with Brynford lessons. I devoured it now for its own sake. Little by little, I acquired Spenser's "Faery Queen," Tasso's "Jerusalem Delivered," Pope's "Iliad," Dryden's "Odyssey," "Paradise Lost," Plutarch's "Lives," Simplicius on

Epictetus, a big "History of the United States," the last of which I sadly needed, because of my utter ignorance of the country I was in.

Mrs. Williams gave me a few empty cases, out of which, with the loan of a saw, hammer, and nails, I constructed a creditable book-case; and, when it was put up, I do believe my senses contained as much delight as they were able to endure, without making me extravagant in behaviour. My attic became my world now, and a very great expansible world, full of kings, emperors, knights, warriors, heroes, and angels. Without, it might have been better, less sordid; within, it was glorious for great deeds and splendid pageantry. It affected my dreams, for I dreamed of the things that I had read. I was transported into Trojan Fields, and Odyssean Isles, and Roman Palaces; and my saturated brain revolved prose as stately as Gibbon's, and couplets that might have been a credit to Pope, only, if I chanced to remember at daybreak what I had been busy upon throughout the night, the metre and rhyme were shameful!

My self-indulgence in midnight readings was hurtful to my eyes, but they certainly interposed between me and other harms. The passion of study was so absorbing that it effectually prevented the intrusion of other passions, while it did not conflict with day-work at the store. Hall and Kemp's young gentlemen sometimes awoke in me a languid interest in Ben de Bar's Theatrical troupe, or in some great actor; but, on reaching home, my little library attracted my attention, and a dip into a page soon effaced all desire for other pleasure.[18] What I am I owe to example, nature, school-education, reading, travel, observation, and reflection. An infinitesimal amount of the mannerisms observed clung to me, no doubt. The housewifely orderliness of Aunt Mary, the serious propriety of Cousin Moses,—then, when I went to sea, the stern voice of the captain, the ripping, explosive manner of the mates, the reckless abandon of the sailors,—after that, the conscientious yielding of myself to details of business,—all this left indelible impressions on me.

About the fourth week Mr. Stanley returned, with a new batch of orders. He warmly congratulated me upon my improved appearance, and

18. McLynn believes that with this fondness for books, indeed HMS's voracious reading itself, "a pathological element began to creep in. His obsession with books as the perfect barrier between himself and the physical world, especially the world of sexuality, became almost fetishistic" (McLynn, *Stanley*, 36).

confidentially whispered to me that Mr. Speake was thoroughly satisfied with my devotion to business. He gave me his card, and said that on the following Sunday he would be glad to see me at breakfast. When the day arrived, I went to St. Charles Street, a quarter greatly superior to St. Thomas Street. The houses were aristocratic, being of classic design, with pillared porticoes, and wide, cool verandas, looking out upon garden-shrubbery and flowering magnolias. Mr. Stanley was in an easy-chair, awaiting me. But for that, I should have hesitated at mounting the wide steps, so imposing the establishment appeared. He took me by the hand to an ample room luxuriously furnished, and introduced me to a fragile little lady, who was the picture of refinement. My reception was of such a character that it led me to believe she was as tender and mild as her quiet and subdued looks; and the books on the centre table made me think her pious. Nothing could have been better calculated to conquer my shyness than the gracious welcome she accorded me. We took our respective places at once, she as a motherly patroness, and I as a devotedly-grateful protégé, fully sensible of what was due to her as the wife of my benefactor. Her husband stood towering over me with his hand on my head, and an encouraging smile on his face, that I might speak out without fear; and he watched the impression I made on his wife. The ordeal of presentation was made easy through her natural goodness, and the gentle art she possessed of winning my confidence. She placed me on a divan near her, and I was soon prattling away with a glibness that a few minutes before would have been deemed impossible to such a stocky boy.

To confine within a sentence my impressions of the first lady I ever conversed with, is entirely beyond my power. There was an atmosphere about her, in the first place, which was wholly new. The elaborateness and richness of dress, the purity and delicacy of her face, the exquisite modulations of her voice, the distinctness of her enunciation, and the sweet courtesy of her manner, I will not say awed me, but it kindled as much of reverence as ever I felt in my life. If I were to combine this with a feeling that the being beside me might command me to endure practically any torture, or dare any danger, for her sake, it will perhaps sum up the effect which this gentlewoman made on my raw mind. It was at this hour I made the discovery of the immense distance between a lady and a mere woman; and, while I gazed at her clear, lustrous eyes, and noted the charms which played about her features, I was thinking that, if a lady could be so superior to an ordinary housewife, with her careless manner of speech, and matter-of-fact ways, what a beautiful thing an angel must be!

When we adjourned to the breakfast-table, I found more material to reflect upon. There were about a dozen people, of about the age and rank of Mr. and Mrs. Stanley, at the table; and it struck me that there was an almost impassable gulf between me and them. Their conversation was beyond my understanding, mostly, though I could spell and interpret each word; but the subjects of their talk left me in the clouds. Their remarks upon literature, politics, and social life, seemed to me most appropriate to books; but it surprised me to think that people could exchange so much learning across a table with the fluency of boys discussing the quality of pudding. Their soothing manner of address, the mutual respect, and deferent temper, greatly elevated them above my coarse-grained acquaintances; and, though they must have guessed, by my manner and age, that I did not belong to their sphere, they paid me the honour of including me in their courteous circle, until, unconsciously, I was straining to acquit myself worthily. Altogether, it was a memorable breakfast; and, when I reached home, it seemed to me that fortune was about to spoil me; otherwise, why this glow and pride that I felt?

After this Sunday, my acquaintance with Mr. Stanley rapidly ripened into something exceeding common gratitude. His bearing towards me was different from that which anybody else showed to me. Many were kind and approving; but, nevertheless, no one stooped to court my notice with that warm, genial manner which distinguished Mr. Stanley. I felt frequently flattered by the encomiums of Mr. Speake, and the friendship of Richardson; but still, there was something of reserve between us, which kept me somewhat tongue-tied in their presence. They never inquired about my welfare or how I liked my boarding-house, or what I thought of anything, or made any suggestion which would stimulate confidence. Their talks with me were all about the business appertaining to the store, or some hap-hazard remark about the weather, or some scene in the street; but Mr. Stanley's way was as though it specially concerned him to know everything about me personally, which had the quality of drawing me out, and making me garrulous, to the verge of familiarity. So, little by little, I came to regard him as an elderly associate, with such a charming, infectious frankness, that I could only, for want of a comparison, remember my affection for my old grandfather, as corresponding with the mixed feelings of regard and awe I had towards him. Besides, to be in his company, even for a brief time, was an education for one so ignorant as myself. Information about somebody or something dropped from his lips with every remark he made. I felt myself becoming intelligent, informed about the geography and history of the city and state that I was in, and learned in the ways and customs of the people. The great merchants and institutions assumed a greater interest for me. They were something more than strange names for repetition; they had associations which revealed personalities of worth, colossal munificence, remunerative enterprise, etc., etc.

Every Sunday morning I spent with the Stanleys, and the instantaneous impression I had received of their goodness was more than confirmed. Mrs. Stanley seemed to become at each visit more tender and caressingly kind, in the same manner as he manifested a more paternal cordiality. I yielded myself wholly to their influence, so that my conduct when out of their sight was governed by the desire to retain their good opinions. Without them, probably, my love of books would have proved sufficient safe-guard against the baser kind of temptations; but, with them, I was rendered almost impregnable to vice. They took me to church, each Sabbath; and, in other ways, manifested a protective care. I resumed the custom of morning and evening prayer, my industry at the store was of a more thoughtful kind, my comings and goings were of more exemplary punctuality. The orderly, industrious life I was following not only ensured me the friendship of the Stanleys, but won me favour from Mr. Speake, who, though wearing often a somewhat anxious expression, restrained himself whenever he had occasion to communicate with me.

In the third month there was a change at the store. Mr. Speake had some words with Mr. Kennicy, the book-keeper, who, being, as I said, touchy, resigned on the spot. A Mr. J. D. Kitchen[19] was employed in his stead, and Mr. Speake saw fit to increase my salary to thirty dollars a month, giving for his reason the fact that the store had never been in such admirable order as it had been since I had entered it. I was immensely proud, of course, at this acknowledgement; but it was only nat-

19. J. D. Kitchen, accountant, is listed in the 1859 City Directory at Nayades and Terpsichore Streets (Gardner, *New Orleans Directory*, 279).

ural that, being so susceptible and impressionable, it should stimulate
me to greater efforts to deserve his approbation. Enlightening me, as it
did, in duties expected of me, it might be said to have increased my interest in the condition of the store, until it partook of that which a fond
proprietor might feel in it. Envious, or ill-natured, people might have
said it was fussy, or officious. At any rate, this disposition to have everything clean, to keep the stacks in orderly arrangement, to be on hand
when wanted, to keep my notes of shipment methodically, to be studi-
ously bent upon perfection in my duties, led to the following incident.

We were ordered to take stock, and, while counting cases, and sacks,
and barrels, etc., I had now and then to rearrange the stacks, because,
in the hurry of business, a box of pickles or jams had become mixed with
biscuits or candle-boxes; and, in handling these articles, it struck me
that several of them were uncommonly light. I mentioned this, but it
did not attract much attention. It was discovered, also, that the coffee-
sacks were much slacker than they ought to be; but, though the rents
through which the contents must have escaped appeared as if made by
rats, as the quantity of berries on the ground was inadequate to the loss,
I knew no other way in which to account for it. However, when, on
going to the lofts, we gauged the contents of the wine-puncheons and
syrup-barrels, and found them to be half-emptied, matters began to
look serious. The leakage on the floor was not sufficient to explain the
loss of so many gallons; and the discussion between the book-keeper
and shipping-clerk suggested trouble when the "old man" would be informed. From what I gathered, the former book-keeper, Mr. Kennicy,
was supposed to be in fault. We were short of several boxes of biscuits,
sardines, and other articles; and it seemed obvious that Mr. Kennicy
must have omitted to enter sales on his book, and thus caused this unexpected discrepancy.

Mr. Speake, as had been anticipated, exhibited much vexation,
though, in the presence of Mr. Kitchen and Mr. Richardson, he could
only ask, querulously, "How could such articles disappear in such a disproportionate manner? We do not sell by retail. If we sold wine, or
syrup, at all, we would sell by the cask, or barrel, and not by the gallon.
The barrels seem to tally, but the contents are diminished in some mysterious manner. Then there are the emptied cases, of which this boy has
spoken: how can we account for bottles taken from one, and tins from
another? The invoices were checked when the goods came in, and no

deficiency was reported to me. There is gross carelessness somewhere, and it must be looked into," etc., etc.

Both Mr. Kitchen and Mr. Richardson, under this argument, laboured under the sense of reproach, and I was not wholly free from a feeling of remissness. I strove hard to remember whether in conveying the cases to their respective piles, or hoisting the barrels to the lofts, a suspicion of light weight had entered my mind; and while filled with a sense of doubt and misgiving, I proceeded to hunt for a broom to sweep up, before closing. I found one in the corner of the back-yard; but, on drawing it to me, a tin lunch-bucket was disclosed, the sight of which in such an unexpected place suggested that the broom had been placed to screen it from view. On taking hold of it, I was amazed at its weight; but, on lifting the lid, I no longer wondered, for it was three-fourths full of golden syrup. It flashed across my mind that here was the solution of the mystery that troubled us, and that, if one bucket was made the means of surreptitiously conveying golden syrup, a second might be used for the same purpose. On searching for the other negro's bucket, I found it placed high above my reach, on a peg, and under his out-door coat. Seizing a board, I struck it underneath, and a few drops of a dark aromatic liquor trickled down the sides. As, now, there could be no reason to doubt that the culprits had been discovered, I hastened to the office to give my information.

By great good-luck, Mr. Stanley appeared at that moment, and I at once acquainted him with what I had found. Mr. Richardson joined us, and, when he had heard it, he became hotly indignant, and cried, "I see it all now. Come on, let us inform Mr. Speake, and have this affair cleared up at once!"

Mr. Speake and Mr. Kitchen were in the office turning over ledger, journal, and day-book, comparing entries, when we burst upon them with the discovery. Mr. Speake was astonished and exclaimed, "There now, who would have thought of these fellows? A systematic robbery has been going on for goodness knows how long!"

While breathlessly discussing the matter, we suddenly remembered various strange proceedings of the negroes, and our suspicions were excited that there must be certain secret nests of stores somewhere in the building; and Richardson and I were sent off to explore. The same idea seemed to be in our minds, for we first searched the dark alleys between the goods-piles, and, in a short time, we had lit upon the secret hoards.

Hams, sardines, and tins of biscuits, packages of candles, etc., etc., were found between the hogsheads and tierces; and, when we had carried them to the office, the indignation of everyone was very high.

Dan and Samuel had been all this time in the upper lofts, and were now called down. When questioned as to their opinions about the disappearance of certain articles, they both denied all knowledge, and affected the ignorance of innocence; but, when they were sharply told to lead us to their tin buckets, their features underwent a remarkable change, and assumed a strange grey colour. Dan pretended to forget where he had placed his bucket; but, when Mr. Speake took him by the collar and led him to the broom that hid it, he fell on his knees, and begged his master's pardon. Mr. Speake was, however, too angry to listen to him, and, snatching the lid off, revealed to us half a gallon of the best golden syrup, which the wretch had intended to have taken home. When Sam's useful utensil was examined, it was found that its owner had a preference for sweet Malmsey wine!

A constable was called in, and Dan and Samuel were marched off to the watch-house, to receive on the next day such a flogging as only practised State-officials know how to administer. Dan, a few days later, was reinstated at the store; but Samuel was disposed of to a planter, for field-work.

The last Sunday morning Mr. Stanley was in the city, on this occasion, was marked with a visit he paid to me at my humble boarding-house. He was pleased to express his great surprise that, at that early hour, my attic was arranged as though for inspection. He scrutinised my book-case, and remarked that I had a pretty broad taste, and suggested that I should procure various books which he mentioned. In self-defence, I was obliged to plead poverty, and explained that my books were only such as I could obtain at a second-hand book-stall. He finally condescended to breakfast with me, and made himself especially agreeable to Mrs. Williams and her guests; after which, we went to church, and thence he took me to dine with him. In the afternoon, we drove in a carriage down Levee Street, past the French Market, and I was shown many of the public buildings, banks, and squares; and, later, we took a short railway trip to Lake Ponchartrain, which is a fair piece of water, and is a great resort for bathers. When we returned to the city, late in the evening, I was fairly instructed in the topography of the city and neighbourhood, and had passed a most agreeable and eventful day.

On the next evening, I found a parcel addressed to me, which, when opened, disclosed a dozen new books in splendid green and blue covers, bearing the names of Shakespeare, Byron, Irving, Goldsmith, Ben Jonson, Cowper, etc. They were a gift from Mr. Stanley, and in each book was his autograph.

The summer of 1859, according to Mr. Richardson, was extremely unhealthy. Yellow fever and dysentery were raging. What a sickly season meant I could not guess; for, in those days, I never read a newspaper, and the city traffic, to all appearance, was much as usual. On Mr. Speake's face, however, I noticed lines of suffering; and one day he was so ill that he could not attend to business. Three or four days later, he was dead; and a message came from the widow that I should visit her, at her home, at the corner of Girod and Carondelet Streets. She was now in a state of terrible distress, and, clad in heavy mourning, she impressed me with very sombre thoughts. It comforted her to hear how sensible we all were of her loss; and then she communicated to me her reasons for desiring my presence. Through her husband she had been made aware of my personal history, and, on account of the interest it had excited in her, she had often induced her husband to tell her every incident at the store. She proceeded to reveal to me the flattering opinion he had formed of me, in terms that augmented my grief; and, as a mark of special favour, I was invited to stay in the house until after the funeral.

That night, I was asked to watch the dead, a duty of which I was wholly unaware before. The body rested in a splendid open coffin, covered with muslin, but the ghastliness of death was somewhat relieved by the Sunday costume in which the defunct merchant was clothed. When the traffic of the streets had ceased, and the silence of the night had fallen on the city, the shadows in the ill-lit room grew mysterious. About midnight, I dozed a little, but suddenly woke up with an instinctive feeling that the muslin had moved! I sprang to my feet, and memories of spectral tales were revived. Was it an illusion, begotten of fear? Was Mr. Speake really dead? There was, at that moment, another movement, and I prepared to give the alarm; but a sacrilegious "meow" betrayed the character of the ghost! A second later, it was felled by a bolster; and, in its haste to escape, the cat entangled its claws in the muslin, and tore and spat in a frenzy; but this was the means of saving

me from the necessity of chasing the wretched animal along the corri-
dors, for, as it was rushing through the door, I caught the veil.

The next day, a long procession wound through the streets towards
the cemetery.[20] The place of interment was surrounded by a high wall,
which contained several square tablets, commemorative, as I supposed,
of the dead lying in the earth; but I was much shocked when I learned
that, behind each tablet, was a long narrow cell wherein bodies were
corrupting. One of these cells had just been opened, and was destined
for the body of my late employer; but, unfortunately for my feelings,
not far off lay, huddled in a corner, the relics of mortality which had
occupied it previously, and which had been ruthlessly displaced.

Within a short time, the store, with all its contents, was disposed of
by auction, to Messrs. Ellison and McMillan. Messrs. Kitchen and
Richardson departed elsewhere, but I was retained by the new firm.
Mrs. Cornelia Speake and her two children removed to Louisville, and
I never saw either of them again.

About this time there came to Mrs. Williams's boarding-house a
blue-eyed and fair-haired lad, of about my own age, seeking lodgings.
As the house was full, the landlady insisted on accommodating him in
my room, and bedding him with me; and, on finding that the boy was
English, and just arrived from Liverpool, I assented to her arrangement.

My intended bed-fellow called himself Dick Heaton, and described
himself as having left Liverpool in the ship *Pocahontas*, as a cabin-boy.
He also had been a victim to the hellish brutality of Americans at sea,
the steward apparently having been as callous and cruel as Nelson of
the *Windermere*; and, no sooner had his ship touched the pier, than the
boy fled, as from a fury. Scarcely anything could have been better calculated to win my sympathy than the recital of experiences similar to my
own, by one of my own age, and hailing from the same port that I had
come from.

Dick was clever and intelligent, though not well educated; but, to
make up for his deficiency in learning, he was gifted with a remarkable

20. DTS quotes from HMS's notebook: "In the morning, hired hack, visited Saint
Roch's, or Campo Santo, St. Louis—1, 2, 3, & 4, Cemeteries—drove to Girod's Ceme-
tery[,] examined book, and found that James Speake died October 26th, and was buried
October 27th, 1859, aged 47" (Stanley, *Autobiography*, 106n).

fluency, and had one of the cheeriest laughs, and a prettiness of manner which made up for all defects.

Our bed was a spacious four-poster, and four slim lads like us might have been easily accommodated in it. I observed, however, with silent surprise, that he was so modest he would not retire by candle-light, and that when he got into bed he lay on the verge of it, far removed from contact with me. When I rose in the morning, I found that he was not undressed, which he explained by saying that he had turned in thus from the habit of holding himself ready for a call. On beginning his voyage he had been so severely thrashed for a delay caused by dressing, that he had scarcely dared to take off his boots during the whole voyage. He also told me that, when he had discovered how almost impossible it was to avoid a beating from the steward and cook, he had resorted to the expedient of padding the seat of his trousers with cotton, and wearing a pad of the same material along the spine, but to avert suspicion that he was thus cunningly fortified against the blows, he had always continued to howl as freely as before. The naïveté of the revelation was most amusing, though I was surprised at the shameless way in which he disclosed his tricks and cowardly fears. However, it did not deter me from responding to his friendly advances, and in two days I came to regard him as a very charming companion. The third morning, being Sunday, we chatted longer abed; but, when rising together, I cast a glance at his hips, and remarked that he need have no fear of being thrashed at New Orleans. He appeared a little confused at first, but, suddenly remembering, he said that on the Monday he would have to purchase a new pair of trousers and seek work. A little later, it struck me that there was an unusual forward inclination of the body, and a singular leanness of the shoulders, compared with the fullness below the waist in him; and I remarked that he walked more like a girl than a boy. "So do you," he retorted, with a liberty natural to our age, at which I only laughed.

I proposed to him that we should breakfast at the French Market that morning, to which he willingly agreed. We walked down Levee Street, down to the foot of Canal Street, where we saw fifty or sixty river steamers assembled, which, massed together, made a most imposing sight. Turning to take a view of the scene up-river, with its miles upon miles of shipping, its levee choked with cotton, and other cargoes, he said that it was a finer sight than even the docks of Liverpool. After a cup of coffee and some sugared waffles, we proceeded on a tour through the old quarter of the city, and wandered past the Cathedral of St. Louis, and through Royal, Chartres, Burgundy, and Toulouse Streets, and, coming home by Rampart Street, entered Canal Street, and continued our weary way, through Carondelet and St. Charles Streets, home, where we arrived heated and hungry. Dick had shown himself very observant, and professed to be astonished at the remarkable variety of complexions and appearance of the population. So long as we were in the neighbourhood of the levee he had been rather shy, and had cast anxious glances about him, fearing recognition from some of the crew of the "Pocahontas"; but, after we had gone into some of the back streets, he had been more at ease, and his remarks upon the types of people we met showed much shrewdness.

Monday morning I woke at an early hour, to prepare myself for the week's labour; and, on looking towards Dick, who was still sound asleep, was amazed to see what I took to be two tumours on his breast. My ejaculation and start woke my companion. He asked what was the matter? Pointing to his open breast, I anxiously inquired if those were not painful?

He reddened, and, in an irritable manner, told me that I had better mind my own business! Huffed at his ungraciousness, I turned resentfully away. Almost immediately after, I reminded myself of his confusion, his strange manner of entering a clean bed with his clothes on, his jealous avoidance of the light, his affectation of modesty, his peculiar suppleness and mincing gait, and the odd style of his figure. These things shaped themselves rapidly into proofs that Dick was not what he represented himself to be. True, he had a boy's name, he wore boy's clothes, he had been a cabin-boy; but such a strange boy I had never seen. He talked far too much and too fluently, he was too tricky, too nimble, somehow. No, I was convinced he could *not* be a boy! I sat up triumphantly and cried out with the delight of a discoverer:—

"I know! I know! Dick, you are a girl!"

Nevertheless, when he faced me, and unblushingly admitted the accusation, it frightened me; and I sprang out of bed as though I had been scorched!

"What," I exclaimed, "do you mean to say you are a girl?"

"Yes, I am," said she, turning pale, as she became infected with my excitement.

Perplexed at this astounding confirmation of what, after all, had been only a surmise of playful malice, I stammeringly demanded,—

"Well, what *is* your name, then? It cannot be Dick, for that belongs to a boy."

"I am Alice Heaton. There, now, you have my whole secret!" she said with asperity

"Alice Heaton!" I echoed, quite confounded at the feminine name; and I reproachfully asked, "If you are a girl, say, what do you mean by coming into my bed, and passing yourself off as a boy?"

She had kept up bravely so far, but she now answered me with tears and sobs, and every doubt of her sex vanished, I was in such a medley of emotions that I stood like one utterly bereft of sense, not knowing what to do. Presently, she said, "Come, let us dress, and I will tell you all about it."

I lost no time in doing what she advised; and, after taking a turn or two in the yard, returned to find her ready for me.

Now that her sex was revealed, I wondered that I had been so blind as not to perceive it before, for, in every movement there was unmistakable femininity. Alice made me sit down, and the substance of the story she now told me was as follows:

She had been born at Everton, Liverpool, and, since she had begun to walk, she had lived with a severe old grandmother who grew more cross as she aged. From childhood, she had known nothing but ill-treatment; she was scolded and slapped perpetually. When she was twelve years of age, she began to struggle with her granny, and, in a short time, she proved that her strength was too great to be beaten by an infirm old woman; little by little, her grandmother desisted from the attempt, but substituted, instead, the nagging system. As she approached her fourteenth year, her grandmother developed a parsimony which made her positively hateful. Every crust she ate at the house was begrudged to her, though, so far as she knew, there was no cause for this pinching and starving. Her home contained evidences of respectability. The furniture was abundant and of good quality, and the many curios in the glass cases in the parlour showed that her parents had been in comfortable circumstances. How her grandmother obtained her means of living, Alice did not know; but, judging from her dress and condition, her poverty was not so distressing as to be the cause of such extreme penuriousness.

During the last five or six months, as she was getting on to fifteen, Alice had been acquainted with girlish neighbours, and through them, with some young middies who had just returned from their voyages. These had delighted to tell her friends of the wonders of foreign lands, and of the genial welcome they had met with from their foreign friends. The stories of their sea-life, and the pictures of America which they gave, fascinated her; and she secretly resolved that, upon the first violent outbreak of her grandmother's temper, she would try her fortune as a cabin-boy. With this view every penny she could scrape, or steal, from her grandmother she hoarded, until, at last, she had enough to purchase from a slop-shop all she needed for a disguise. When her grandmother finally broke out into a bad fit of temper, and, provoked by her defiance, ordered her out of the house, she was ready for her venture. She went to a barber's shop and had her hair cut close; returning home, she dressed herself in boy's costume, and, with a sailor's bag on her back, entered a boarding-house near the docks. A few days later, she had the good luck to be engaged as a cabin-boy by the captain of the *Pocahontas*, and, by careful conduct, escaped detection during the voyage, though nothing would avail her to avoid the rope's ending and cuffing of the steward and his fellow-officers.

By the time she had concluded her narrative, it was full time for me to depart to my work. We hurriedly agreed to consult together about future plans upon my return in the evening, and I left her with an assurance that all my means and help were at her service. All that day her extraordinary story occupied my mind, and, though she was undoubtedly an artful and bold character, her uncommon spirit compelled my admiration, while her condition was such as to compel my sympathy. At the closing hour I sped homeward, but, on arriving at Mrs. Williams's, I was told Alice had not been seen since the early morning. I waited many hours, but waited in vain. She was never seen, or heard of, by me again; but I have hoped ever since that Fate was as propitious to her, as I think it was wise, in separating two young and simple creatures, who might have been led, through excess of sentiment, into folly.[21]

21. McLynn dismisses the story of Alice as "fantasy derived from the Shakespearian comedies [HMS] was reading at the time. But there is a more profound meaning for the fantasy. It is utterly implausible for a former inmate at St. Asaph's to tell us, as Stanley does, that he knew nothing of female anatomy and had never seen a girl's breasts before. The true significance of the tale is Stanley's uncertainty about *his own* sexual identity."

The next Sabbath after the disappearance of Alice, I paid my usual visit to Mrs. Stanley, and was shocked and grieved to hear, from her maid, Margaret, that she was seriously ill, and under medical treatment. A glass of ice-water which she had taken on Friday had been speedily followed by alarming symptoms of illness. She was now so prostrated by disease that she required constant attendance. Margaret's face betrayed so much fatigue and anxiety that I tendered my services, and even begged her to employ me in any way. After a little hesitation, she said I might be useful in enabling her to take a little rest, if I would sit at the door, and, upon any movement or sound within the sick chamber, call her. I kept my post all through the day and night, and, though there were frequent calls on Margaret, her snatches of rest served to maintain her strength. As I went off to my labour, I promised to solicit a few days' leave from Mr. Ellison, and to return to her within the hour.

Mr. Ellison, however, to whom I preferred my request for a few days' liberty, affected to regard me as though I had uttered something very outrageous, and curtly told me I "might go to the D——, if I liked, and stay with him for good." Such an offensive reply, a few months earlier, would have made me shrink into myself; but the New Orleans atmosphere ripens one's sense of independence and personal dignity, and I replied with something of the spirit that I had admired in Mr. Kennicy and Mr. Richardson, and said:—

"Very well, sir. You may discharge me at once!" Of course, to a person of Mr. Ellison's sanguinary hair and complexion, the answer was sufficient to ensure my furious dismissal on the instant.

Margaret was greatly vexed at my action when she heard of it, but consoled me by saying that a few days' liberty would do me no harm. My whole time was now placed at her disposal, and I had reason to know that my humble services were a considerable relief and assistance to her at this trying time. Meanwhile, poor Mrs. Stanley was becoming steadily worse; and, on Wednesday night, her case was reported to be desperate by the physician. There was no more sleep for any of us until the issue should be decided. Near midnight, Margaret, with a solemn and ghastly face, beckoned me into the sick lady's room. With my heart

Bierman, although more inclined to believe HMS's story, hedges by stating that Alice is reminiscent of Sweet Polly Oliver, "a familiar folkloric figure of the eighteenth and nineteenth centuries" (McLynn, *Stanley*, 36; Bierman, *Dark Safari*, 18).

throbbing painfully, and expecting I know not what, I entered on tiptoe. I saw a broad bed, curtained with white muslin, whereon lay the fragile figure of the patient so frail and delicate that, in my rude health, it seemed insolence in me to be near her. It had been easy for me to speak of illness when I knew so little of what it meant; but, on regarding its ravages, and observing the operation of death, I stood as one petrified.

Margaret pushed me gently to the bedside, and I saw by the dim light how awfully solemn a human face can be when in saintly peace. Slowly, I understood how even the most timid woman could smilingly welcome Death, and willingly yield herself to its cold embrace. I had hitherto a stony belief that those who died had only been conquered through a sheer want of will on their part ("All men think all men mortal but themselves"),[22] and that the monster, with its horrors of cold, damp earth, and worms, needed only to be defied to be defeated of its prey. While listening at the door, I had wished that, in some way, I could transfuse a portion of my fullness of spirit into her, that she might have the force to resist the foe; for, surely, with a little more courage, she would not abandon husband, friends, and admirers, for the still company in the Churchyard. But the advance of Death was not like that of a blustering tyrant. It was imperceptible, and inconceivably subtle, beginning with a little ache—like one of many known before. Before it had declared its presence, it had narcotized the faculties, eased the beats of the heart, lessened the flow of blood, weakened the pulse; it had sent its messenger, Peace, before it, to dispel all anxieties and regrets, and to elevate the soul with the hope of Heaven; and then it closed the valves.

She opened her mild eyes, and spoke words as from afar: "Be a good boy. God bless you!" And, while I strained my hearing for more, there was an indistinct murmur, the eyes opened wide and became fixed, and a beautiful tranquillity settled over the features. How strangely serene! When I turned to look into Margaret's eyes, I knew Death had come.

By a curious coincidence; Captain Stanley, her brother-in-law, arrived from Havana the next day, in a brig.[23] He knew nothing of me. There was no reason he should be tender to my feelings, and he intimated to me, with the frankness of a ship's captain, that he would take

22. Edward Young, *Night Thoughts on Life, Death, and Immortality*, book I, line 424.
23. HMS probably refers to HHS's half-brother James Howard Brooks of Manchester, England.

charge of everything. Even Margaret subsided before this strong man; and, being very miserable, and with a feeling of irretrievable loss, I withdrew, after a silent clasp of the hands.

About three days later I received a letter from Margaret, saying that the body had been embalmed, and the casket had been put in lead; and that, according to a telegram received from Mr. Stanley, she was going up the river to St. Louis with it, by the steamer *Natchez*.

For a period, I was too forlorn to heed anything greatly. I either stayed at home, reading, or brooding over the last scene in Mrs. Stanley's chamber, or I wandered aimlessly about the levee, or crossed over to Algiers,[24] where I sat on the hulks, and watched the river flowing, with a feeling as of a nightmare on me.[25]

My unhappy experiences at Liverpool had not been without their lessons of prudence. My only extravagances so far had been in the purchase of books; and, even then, a vague presentiment of want had urged me to be careful, and hurry to raise a shield against the afflictions of the destitute. Though at liberty, there was no fear that I should abuse it.

By and by, the cloud lifted from my mind; and I set about seeking for work. Fortune, however, was not so kind this time. The Mr. Stanleys of the world are not numerous. After two weeks' diligent search, there was not a vacancy to be found. Then I lowered my expectations, and sought for work of any kind. I descended to odd jobs, such as the sawing of wood, and building wood-piles for private families. The quality of the work mattered little.

One day there came a mate to our boarding-house, who told me that his captain was ill, and required an attendant. I offered myself, and was accepted.

The vessel was the *Dido*, a full-sized brig. The captain suffered from a bilious fever, aggravated by dysentery, from drinking Mississippi water, it was thought. He was haggard, and yellow as saffron. I received my instructions from the doctor, and committed them to paper to prevent mistakes.

24. The little town of Algiers was located just below New Orleans, across the Mississippi River on the west (south) bank.

25. The story of Mrs. Stanley's death is a "tissue of lies," declares McLynn. "Henry Hope Stanley's wife did *not* die in 1859 but on 9 April 1878, aged forty-six, in New Orleans" (McLynn, *Stanley*, 37). Frances Stanley's obituary appeared April 9 and 10, 1878, in the *New Orleans Daily Picayune*.

My duties were light and agreeable. During the remission of fever, the captain proved to be a kindly and pious soul; and his long grey beard gave him a patriarchal appearance, and harmonized with his patient temper. For three weeks we had an anxious time over him, but, during the fourth, he showed signs of mending, and took the air on the poop. He became quite communicative with me, and had extracted from me mostly all that was worth relating of my short history.

At the end of a month I was relieved from my duties; and as I had no desire to resume sea-life, even with so good a man, I was paid off most handsomely, with a small sum as a "token of regard." As I was about to depart, he said some words which, uttered with all solemnity, were impressive. "Don't be down-hearted at this break in the beginning of your life. If you will only have patience, and continue in well-doing, your future will be better than you dream of. You have uncommon faculties, and I feel certain that, barring accidents, you will some day be a rich man. If I were you, I would seek your friend at St. Louis, and what you cannot find in this city, you may find in that. You deserve something better than to be doing odd jobs. Good-bye, and take an old man's best wishes."

The old captain's words were better than his gold, for they gave me a healthful stimulus. His gold was not to be despised, but his advice inspired me with hope, and I lifted my head, and fancied I saw clearer and further. All men must pass through the bondage of necessity before they emerge into life and liberty. The bondage to one's parents and guardians is succeeded by bondage to one's employers.

On the very next day I took a passage for St. Louis, by the steamer *Tuscarora*; and, by the end of November, 1859, I reached that busy city. The voyage had proved to me wonderfully educative. The grand pictures of enterprise, activity, and growing cities presented by the river shores were likely to remain with me forever. The successive revelations of scenery and human life under many aspects impressed me with the extent of the world. Mental exclamations of "What a river!" "What a multitude of steamers!" "What towns, and what a people!" greeted each new phase. The intensity of everything also surprised me, from the resistless and deep river, the driving force within the rushing boats, the galloping drays along the levees, to the hurried pace of everybody ashore. On our own steamer my nerves tingled incessantly with the sound of the fast-whirling wheels, the energy of the mates, and the clamour of the hands. A feverish desire to join in the bustle burned in my veins.

On inquiring at the Planters' Hotel, I extracted from the hotel clerk the news that Mr. Stanley had descended to New Orleans on business a week before! For about ten days I hunted for work along the levee, and up and down Broadway, and the principal streets, but without success; and, at last, with finances reduced to a very low ebb, the river, like a magnet, drew me towards it. I was by this time shrunk into a small compass, even to my own perception. Self-depreciation could scarcely have become lower.

Wearied and disheartened, I sat down near a number of flat-boats and barges, several of which were loading, or loaded, with timber, boards, and staves; and the talk of the men,—rough-bearded fellows,— about me, was of oak, hickory, pine shingles, scantling, and lumber; and I heard the now familiar names of Cairo, Memphis, and New Orleans. At the last word, my attention was aroused, and I discovered that one of the flat-boats was just about to descend the river to that port. Its crew were seated on the lumber, yarning lightheartedly; and their apparent indifference to care was most attractive to an outcast. I stole nearer to them, found out the boss, and, after a while, offered to work my passage down the river. Something in me must have excited his rough sympathy, for he was much kinder than might have been expected from his rough exterior. I had long since learned that the ordinary American was a curious compound of gentleman and navvy.[26] His garb and speech might be rough, his face and hands soiled, beard and hair unkempt, but the bearing was sure to be free, natural, and grand, and his sentiments becoming; the sense of manly dignity was never absent, and his manners corresponded with his situation. My services were accepted, not without receiving a hint that loafing could not be tolerated aboard a flat-boat. Being the youngest on board, I was to be a general helper, assist the cook, and fly about where wanted. But what a joy to the workless is occupation! Independence may be a desirable thing, but the brief taste I had had of it had, by this, completely sickened me.

We cast off at day-break, and committed our huge unwieldy boat to the current of the Mississippi, using our sweeps occasionally to keep her in the middle. For the most part it seemed to me a lazy life. The physi-

26. A British term for an unskilled laborer.

cal labours were almost nil, though, now and then, all hands were called to exert their full strength, and the shouting and swearing were terrific. When the excitement was passed, we subsided into quietude, smoking, sleeping, and yarning. A rude galley had been set up temporarily for the cook's convenience, and a sail was stretched over the middle of the boat as a shelter from the sun and rain. There were eleven of us altogether, including myself. My promiscuous duties kept me pretty busy. I had to peel potatoes, stir mush, carry water, wash tin pans, and scour the plates, and on occasions lend my strength at pulling one of the tremendously long oars. No special incident occurred during the long and tedious voyage. Once we narrowly escaped being run down by the *Empress* steamer, and we had a lively time of it, the angry men relieving themselves freely of threats and oaths. Steamers passed us every day. Sometimes a pair of them raced madly side by side, or along opposite banks, while their furnaces, fed by pitch-pine, discharged rolling volumes of thick smoke, which betrayed, for hours after they had disappeared from view, the course they had taken. The water would splash up the sides of our boat, and the yellow river would part into alarming gulfs on either hand. At large towns, such as Cairo, Memphis, Vicksburg, and Natchez, we made fast to the shore; and, while the caterer of the mess took me with him to make his purchases of fresh provisions, the crew sought congenial haunts by the river-side for a mild dissipation. By the end of the month, our voyage terminated at some stave and lumber-yards between Carrolltown and New Orleans.

On the whole, the flat-boatmen had been singularly decent in their behaviour. Their coarseness was not disproportionate to their circumstances, or what might be expected from wage-earners of their class; but what impressed me most was the vast amount of good feeling they exhibited. There had been a few exciting tussles, and some sharp exchanges of bellicose talk between the principals, but their bitterness vanished in a short time, while, towards myself, they were more like protectors than employers. Nevertheless, a few painful truths had been forced on my notice; I had also gained valuable experience of the humours of rivers. The fluvial moods had considerably interested me. The play of currents, eddies, and whirlpools afforded inexhaustible matter for observation. The varying aspects of the stream in calm and storm, when deep or shallow, in the neighbourhood of snags, sandbars, and spits, reflecting sunshine or leaden sky, were instructive, and the veteran flat-boatmen were not averse to satisfying my inquisitiveness. Being naturally studious and reflective, I carried away with me far more than I could rehearse of what was of practical value; but, boy-like, I relegated my impressions to memory, where, in process of time, they could be solidified into knowledge.

3

I Find a Father

After tying up, I was at liberty to renovate my person. My shore-clothes restored me to the semblance of my former self, and, with many a protest of good-will from my late companions, I walked towards the city. In a few hours I reached St. Charles Street, and, as though wearied with its persecution of me, Fortune brought me into the presence of Mr. Stanley. His reception of me was so paternal that the prodigal son could not have been more delighted. My absence from New Orleans had but intensified my affection for the only friend I seemed to possess in all America. Once out of his presence, I felt as a stranger among strangers; on re-entering it, I became changed outwardly and inwardly. Away from him, I was at once shy, silent, morosely severe; with him, I was exuberantly glad, and chatted freely, without fear of repulse. Since we had parted, I had met some thousands, and spoken with a few hundreds; but no one had kindled in me the least spark of personal interest. It may, then, be understood how my greeting expressed my sense of his preeminence and rarity.

Between the last sentence and what follows, there should be an interval represented by many * * * * I do know how it came about, but I was suddenly fixed immovably, for a period. Preoccupied with my bursting gladness, I had observed nothing but our mutual gratification; and then I had poured my tale of woes unchecked, except by expression of sympathy, now and again, from him. But, presently, after some commonplaces, his words sounded a deeper note, and stirred my innermost being. A peculiar sensation—as though the wind of a strong breathing was flowing down my back, and ran up with a refluent motion to the head, blowing each hair apart—came over me, and held me spellbound and thrilled to the soul. *He was saying, with some emotion, that my future should be his charge!* He had been so powerfully affected by what Margaret had told him, with all the warmth of her Irish nature, of the last scene at the deathbed of his wife, that he had been unable to dissociate me from his thoughts of her; he had wondered what I was doing, what had become of me, imagined that I was starving, and, knowing how friendless and unsophisticated I was, each conjecture had been dismal and pitiful; and he had resolved, on reaching New Orleans, to make diligent search for me, and take me to himself. While he related his extraordinary intentions, it seemed to me as if my spirit was casting an interested regard upon my own image, and was glorying in the wonderful transformation that was taking place. To think that any man should be weaving such generous designs upon a person so unworthy and insignificant as myself, and plotting a felicitous future for me, nursed in contumely and misery, seemed to me to be too wonderful for belief! Then, again, there was a certain mysterious coincidence about it which awed me. In my earliest dreams and fancies, I had often imagined what kind of a boy I should be with a father or mother. What ecstasy it would be if my parent came to me, to offer a parent's love, as I had enviously seen it bestowed on other children. In my secret prayers, something of a wish of this kind had been behind the form of words; and now, as an answer from the Invisible, came this astounding revelation of His power! He had cast a little leaven of kindness into the heart of a good man. From the very first encounter, it had acted beneficially for me; and now it had leavened his whole nature, until it had become a fatherly affection, which would shield my youth from trial and temptation, and show me the best side of human nature!

Before I could quite grasp all that this declaration meant for me, he had risen, taken me by the hand, and folded me in a gentle embrace. My senses seemed to whirl about for a few half-minutes: and, finally, I broke down, sobbing from extreme emotion. It was the only tender action I had ever known, and, what no amount of cruelty could have forced from me, tears poured in a torrent under the influence of the simple embrace.

The golden period of my life began from that supreme moment! As I glance back at it from the present time, it seems more like a dream, as unreal as a vision of the night. Compared with these matter-of-fact days, or the ruthless past, it was like a masquerade among goodly felicities and homely affections, and its happy experiences have been too precious and sacred for common chat, though they have lain near enough for the fitting occasion, moulded and ready for utterance. They have formed my best memories, and furnished me with an unfading store of reflections, and, probably, have had more influence than any other upon my conduct and manners.[1] For, to be lifted out of the depths of friendlessness and destitution to a paternal refuge, and made the object of care and solicitude so suddenly, at a time, too, when I was most impressionable, without an effort on my own part, and without an advocate, bordered on the miraculous. Predisposed to inward communing, with a strong but secret faith in Providence, I regarded it as principally the result of Divine interposition, the course of which was a mystery not to be lightly talked of, but to be remembered for its significance.

After a restful night, and when breakfast had been despatched, we adjourned to a room used as an office and sitting apartment, and there I was subjected to a sympathetic cross-examination. Every incident of my life, even to the fancies that had fled across the mind of callow boyhood, was elicited with the assistance of his searching questions, and then I was, as it were, turned completely inside out. Mr. Stanley said that what I had told him only bore out the conclusion he had long before arrived at concerning me. He had suspected that I was an orphan, or one who had been flatly disowned, and a waif exposed to every wind of Chance; and he was glad that it had deposited me in his keeping. He expressed amazement that helpless children were treated so unfeelingly in England, and marvelled that no one cared to claim them. Being a childless man, he and his wife had often prayed for the blessing of offspring, until they were wearied with desiring and expecting. Then they had gone to the Faubourg St. Mary and had visited the Infant Asylum, with the view of adopting some unclaimed child; but they had made no choice, from over-fastidiousness. It much surprised him that none of my relations had discovered in me what had struck him and Speake.

---

1. Despite all the evident inaccuracies and fabrications surrounding his relationship with Mr. and Mrs. Stanley, HMS appears deeply sincere. Could these kind delusions have supplanted actual memory of the events and individuals? It seems incredulous that HMS, the consummate man of action, could have and would have gone to such elaborate lengths to mix such whitewash.

Had he searched New Orleans all through, he said, he could not have found one who would have shared his views respecting me with more sympathy than his friend; and, had Mr. Speake lived, he added, I should have been as good as established for life. Mr. Speake had written his estimates of my character often, and, in one letter, had predicted that I was cut out for a great merchant, who would eventually be an honour to the city. Mr. Kitchen, the book-keeper, had also professed to be impressed with my qualities; while young Richardson had said I was a prodigy of activity and quick grasp of business.

Then, at some length, he related the circumstances which had induced him to take a warmer interest in me. He had often thought of the start I had given him by the question, "Do you want a boy, sir?" It seemed to voice his own life-long wish. But he thought I was too big for his purpose. For the sake, however, of the long-desired child, he determined to do the best he could for me, and had obtained my engagement with his friend Speake. When he had gone home, his wife had been much interested in the adventure with me, and had often asked how his "protégé" was getting on? When she had, finally, seen me, she had said something to him which had given a new turn to his thoughts; but, as I was already established, and was likely to succeed, he had ceased thinking about it. On Margaret's arrival at St. Louis with his wife's remains,[2] she had been so eloquent in all the details of what had occurred, that he inwardly resolved that his first object on reaching the city should be to seek me and undertake what God had pointed out to him; namely, to educate me for the business of life, and be to me what my father should have been. "The long and the short of it is," said he, "as you are wholly unclaimed, without a parent, relation, or sponsor, I promise to take you for my son, and fit you for a mercantile career; and, in future, *you are to bear my name, Henry Stanley*." Having said which, he rose, and, dipping his hands in a basin of water, he made the sign of the cross on my forehead, and went seriously through the formula of baptism, ending with a brief exhortation to bear my new name worthily.[3]

2. It appears indisputable that Frances Meller Stanley did not die in late 1859, as Stanley relates, but almost twenty years later (see n. 25 in chapter 2).

3. "For Henry Hope Stanley's purported adoption of John Rowlands, not a scrap of documentary evidence can be found, and indeed the explorer himself gives no account of any formal or legal measures having been taken in this direction, beyond the patently

In answer, as it might seem, to the least shade of doubt on my face, which he thought he observed, he gave me a brief summary of his own life, from which I learned that he had not always been a merchant. He told me that he had been educated for the ministry, and had been ordained,[4] and for two years had preached in various places between Nashville and Savannah; but, finally, becoming lukewarm, he had lost his original enthusiasm for his profession, and had turned his attention to commerce. Intimacy with men of business, and social life, had led him by degrees to consider himself unfitted for a calling which seemed to confine his natural activities; but, though he had lost the desire to expound the Christian faith from the pulpit, he had not lost his principles. The greater gains of commerce had seemed to him to be more attractive than the work of persuading men and women to be devout. After one or two unsuccessful essays as a store keeper, he had finally adopted a commission business, and had succeeded in several profitable ventures. He thought that, in a few years, he would return to the store business, and settle in "one of the back-country places" for which he had a great hankering; but, at present, he could not make up his mind to terminate his city connections. Much else he related to me, for it was a day of revelations; but to me, personally, it mattered little—it was quite sufficient that he was he, my first, best friend, my benefactor, my father!

Only the close student of the previous pages could compass my feelings at finding the one secret wish of my heart gratified so unexpectedly. To have an unbreathed, unformed wish plucked out of the silence, and fashioned into a fact as real as though my dead father had been restored to life and claimed me, was a marvel so great that I seemed to be divided into two individuals—one strenuously denying that such a thing could be, and the other arraying all the proofs of the fact. It was even more of a wonder than that Dick the boy should be transformed into Alice the girl! But when hour after hour passed, and each brought its substantial evidence of the change, the disturbed faculties gradually returned to their normal level, though now more susceptible to happiness than when existence was one series of mortifications.

---

spurious 'baptismal' ceremony described in his autobiography" (Bierman, *Dark Safari*, 27).

4. "He was never ordained, although his mother had, after the death of her first husband, been re-married to a Presbyterian clergyman" (Hall, *Stanley*, 122).

As we walked the streets together, many a citizen must have guessed by my glowing face and shining eyes that I was brimful of joy. I began to see a new beauty in everything. The men seemed pleasanter, the women more gracious, the atmosphere more balmy! It was only by severe suppression that I was able to restrain myself from immoderate behaviour, and breaking out into hysteric and unseemly ebullience. A gush of animal enjoyment in life, from this date, would sometimes overtake me, and send me through the streets at the rate of a professional pedestrian. I would open my mouth and drink the air, with deep disdain for all physical weakness. I had to restrain the electrical vitality, lest the mad humour for leaping over a dray or cart might awaken the suspicion of the policeman. On such days, and during such fits, it was indeed joy to be alive,—"but to be young was very Heaven."[5]

Most of the day was spent in equipping me for the new position I was to assume. I was sumptuously furnished with stylish suits, new linen, collars, flannels, low-quarter shoes, and kip[6] boots: toilet articles to which I was an utter stranger, such as tooth-and-nail-brushes, and long white shirts, resembling girls' frocks, for night-dresses. It had never entered my head, before, that teeth should be brushed, or that a nail-brush was indispensable, or that a night-dress contributed to health and comfort! When we returned to Mr. Stanley's boarding-house, we had a pleasant time in the arrangement of the piles of new garments and accessories, and in practising the first lessons in the art of personal decoration. In Wales the inhabitants considered it unbecoming in one who aspired to manliness to ape the finicky niceties of women, and to be too regardful of one's personal appearance; and had they heard my new father descant so learnedly on the uses of tooth-and-nail-brushes, I feel sure they would have turned away with grimaces and shrugs of dissatisfaction. What would stern Aunt Mary have said, had she viewed this store of clothing and linen that was destined for the use of a boy whom, at one time, she had seriously meditated indenturing to a cobbler? But, previous to the assumption of my new habiliments, I was conducted to a long bath, set in a frame of dark wood, and, while looking at it, and wondering at its splendour, I heard so many virtues ascribed to its daily use that I contracted quite a love for it, and vowed to myself

5. William Wordsworth, *The Prelude*, book 2, line 108.
6. DTS's note: "A special kind of leather" (Stanley, *Autobiography*, 123n).

that since it appeared to be a panacea for so many ills, all that scented soap and scrubbing could effect would be gladly tested by me.

I steeped myself that afternoon, as though I would wash out the stains ugly poverty and misery had impressed upon my person since infancy; and, when I emerged out of the bath, my self-esteem was as great as befitted the name and character I was hereafter to assume.[7] But there was much to improve inwardly as well as outwardly. The odium attached to the old name, and its dolorous history, as it affected my sense of it, could not be removed by water, but by diligent application to a moral renovation, and making use of the new life, with the serious intent to hold the highest ideal I knew of, as my exemplar. To aid me in my endeavours, my new father was gentleness itself. At first, he made no great demand on me; but our intercourse was permitted to grow to that familiar intimacy which inspired perfect confidence. There was no fear that I could ever be contemptuous or disrespectful; but, had he not allowed a certain time for familiarising me with his presence and position towards me, I might not have been able to overcome a natural timidity which would have ill-suited our connection. When I had learned to touch him without warning, and yet receive a genial welcome, laugh in his presence unchecked, and even comb his beard with my fingers, then I came completely out of my shell; and, after that, development was rapid.

"Boys should be seen, and not heard," had been so frequently uttered before me that I had grown abashed at the sound of an adult's voice. The rule was now agreeably reversed. I was encouraged to speak upon every occasion, and to utter my opinions regardless of age and sex. No incident occurred, and no subject was mentioned, that I was not invited to say what I thought of it.

Apart from commercial and cognate details, I think my ripening understanding was made more manifest in anything relating to human in-

7. Although HMS would use the name Henry Stanley at once, it would be at least ten years before he settled on "Morton" as his middle name. In the meantime he employed "Morelake" and "Morley." Even David Livingstone, in his journal, referred to HMS as Henry Moreland Stanley. In the 1860 census, however, HMS gave his name as William H. Stanley and used this name when he enlisted in the Confederate Army the following year. When he was captured at Shiloh, HMS gave his name as simply H. Stanley and as such he is listed in Federal prison records (McLynn, *Stanley*, 335, 7n; 1860 Census of Arkansas County, Arkansas, HH 599).

tercourse and human nature, owing, probably, to the greater efforts
made by my father to assist me in recovering lost ground. Boys bred up
at home pick up instinctively, the ways and manners prevailing there. I
had had no home, and therefore I was singularly deficient in the little
graces of home life. Unconsciously to myself, from the moment I had
stepped out of the bath-room in my new garments, I began that elementary education which was to render me fit to be seen by the side of
a respectable man. I had to lose the fear of men and women, to know
how to face them without bashfulness or awkwardness, to commune
with them without slavish deference, to bear myself without restraint,
and to carry myself with the freedom which I saw in others; in a word,
I had to learn the art of assimilating the manner, feeling, and expression
of those around me. Being attentive and intelligent, acute of hearing,
quick of eye-sight, and with a good memory, I had gained immensely
in my father's estimation, and he was, to me, a sufficient judge.

Our wanderings from city to city, steamer to steamer, and store to
store, which the business of my father necessitated, I do not propose to
dwell upon; in fact, it would be impossible to contain within a volume
all that I remember of this, and subsequent periods. I am more concerned with the personal element, the cardinal incidents, and the trac-
ing of my growth to maturity. Besides, the banks of the Mississippi and
its lower tributaries have little to recommend them to a youngster after
the first expressive Oh! of admiration. The planters' mansions, the settlements, and cities, are mainly of uniform colour and style of architecture. When we have seen one mansion, settlement, or city, we seem to
have seen all. One river-bank is like the other. The houses are either of
wood with a verandah, and painted, or of red brick; there is a church
spire here, and, there, a mass of buildings; but presently, after a second
view, there is as little of lasting interest as in the monotonous shores of
the great river. I only record such incidents as affected me, and such as
clearly stand out conspicuously in the retrospect, which have been not
only a delight to memory, but which I am incapable of forgetting.

During nearly two years, we travelled several times between New
Orleans, St. Louis, Cincinnati, and Louisville; but most of our time was
spent on the lower Mississippi tributaries, and on the shores of the
Washita, Saline, and Arkansas Rivers, as the more profitable commissions were gained in dealings with country merchants between Harris-
onburg and Arkadelphia, and between Napoleon and Little Rock. From

these business tours I acquired a better geographical knowledge than any amount of school-teaching would have given me; and at one time I was profound in the statistics relating to population, commerce, and navigation of the Southern and South-Western States. Just as Macaulay was said to be remarkable for being able to know a book from beginning to end by merely turning over its pages, I was considered a prodigy by my father and his intimate friends for the way names and faces clung to my memory. I could tell the name of every steamer we had passed, the characteristics of her structure, and every type of man we met. A thing viewed, or a subject discussed likely to be useful, became impressed indelibly on the mind. Probably this mental acquisitiveness was stimulated by the idea that it formed the equipment of a merchant, which I believed it was my ultimate destiny to be; and that every living man should be a living gazetteer, and possess facts and figures at his fingers' ends. Meantime, my memory was frequently of great use to my father as an auxiliary to his memorandum-book of shipments, purchases, and sales. Once having seen the page, I could repeat its record with confidence; and I was often rewarded by his admiring exclamation, "Well, I never heard the like! It is perfectly astonishing how you remember details," etc. But, though eyes and ears and technical memory were well exercised, it was some time before judgement was formed. Understanding was slow. It took long for me to perceive wherein lay the superiority of one sugar over another, or why one grade of flour fetched a higher price than another, or wherein Bourbon whiskey was superior to rye, and to distinguish the varying merits of coffees, teas, etc. What a man said, or how he looked, his dress, appearance, and so on, were ineffaceable; but the unwritten, or untold, regarding him was a blank to me; and when I heard comments from bystanders upon the nature of some person, I used to wonder how they formed their opinions. However, the effect of these criticisms upon men and their manners was to inspire me with a desire to penetrate beneath, and to school myself in comparing different people. I had abundance of opportunities, in the multitudes we met in the crowded steamers, and the many towns we visited; but that which would have given the key to the mystery was wanting, viz., personal intercourse. In the absence of direct conversation and dealings with people, it was difficult to discover the nature of a spirit lurking under a fair outside.

When we left New Orleans, at the end of 1859,[8] we had brought with us a portmanteau packed with choice literature, and I was given to understand that the histories of Rome, Greece, and America, poetry and drama, were especially for my use, and that I was to pursue my studies as diligently as at a school. The practice of travel enabled my father to dispose himself comfortably for the indulgence of reading, within a very short time after reaching his cabin. He acted as one who had only changed his room, and was only concerned with his own business. With such a man, a river-voyage was no impediment to instruction. He set me an example of application to my book, which, added to my own love of study, enabled me to cultivate indifference to what was passing outside of our cabin. Our travelling library was constantly replenished at the large cities, with essays, memoirs, biographies, and general literature; but novels and romances were rigidly excluded.

He first taught me how a book should be read aloud, and, in a few seconds, had corrected a sing-song intonation which was annoying to him. He said that one could almost tell whether a reader understood his author by the tone of his delivery; and, taking up a Shakespeare, he illustrated it by reading, "Who steals my purse steals trash,"[9] etc.; and the various styles he adopted were well calculated to enforce his lesson. From the monotone I was unable to see any beauty or point in the quotation; but, when he assumed the tone of the moralist, the lines certainly set me thinking, and the truth of the sentiments appeared so clear that I was never able to forget the quotation.

Sometimes, also, when reading aloud a page of history, I would come to a dull paragraph, and my attention would flag; but he was quick to detect this, and would compel me to begin again, because he was sure that I knew not what I had been reading. I merely note this because during two years we read together a large number of books and, as I had the benefit of his disquisitions and comments on my reading, it will be

8. The reader will recall that earlier in this chapter HMS states that he and his father, for "nearly two years," traveled up and down the Mississippi and the Ohio. This cannot be reconciled with the 1860 census showing young Stanley at Cypress Bend in the household of Isaac Altshur in mid-August. Even "by his own account—the young Stanley arrived in Cypress Bend at least a year earlier, in January 1861" (1860 Census of Arkansas County, Arkansas, HH 599, Douglas township, South Bend post office; Bierman, *Dark Safari*, 27–28).

9. The words of Iago (*Othello*, act 3, scene 3, line 155).

seen that with such a companion these river-voyages considerably advanced my education, as much so, indeed, as though I had been with a tutor. Nor, when we dropped our books, and promenaded the deck, was my mind left to stagnate in frivolity. He took advantage of every object worthy of notice to impress on me some useful, or moral lesson,—to warn me against errors of omission, or commission.

Whatever it may have been in my personal appearance that first attracted him to me, it is certain that the continued affection he always showed towards me was secured by my zealous efforts always to follow his slightest suggestion. I think it would have been difficult to have found a boy in the neighbourhood of the Mississippi who observed his parent's wishes with a more scrupulous exactitude than I did those of my adopted father. As I came to have an entire knowledge of him, I knew not which to admire most, the unvarying, affectionate interest he showed in my personal welfare, or his merits as a man and moral guardian. Being of original ideas, acute mind, and impressive in speech, the matter of his conversation glued itself into my memory, and stirred me to thought.

I remember well when, one day, he revealed something of the method he proposed to follow with me for the perfecting of my commercial education, I expressed doubt as to whether, after all his trouble and care, I would ever come up to his expectations. I said that as to carrying out plain instructions with all good-will there need be no fear—I loved work, and the approbation given to fidelity and industry; but, when I contemplated being left to my own judgement, I felt strong misgivings. How admirably he interpreted my thoughts, explained my doubts! He infused me with such confidence that, had a store been given me there and then, I should have instantly accepted its management! "But," he said, "I am not going to part with you yet. You have much to learn. You are a baby in some things yet, because you have been only a few months in the world. By the time I have wound up matters, you will have learned thousands of little trifles, and will be so grounded in solid knowledge that you may safely be trusted under another merchant to learn the minutiae of business, and so get ready to keep store with me."

I suggested to him that I laboured under disadvantages such as hampered very few other boys, which would act as a clog on the free exercise of my abilities, and that, even if other people refrained from alluding to my Parish breeding, the memory of it would always have a depressing effect on me. But such thoughts he met with something like angry contempt. "I don't know," said he, "what the custom of the Welsh people may be, but *here* we regard personal character and worth, not pedigree. With us, people are advanced, not for what their parentage may have been, but for what they are themselves. All whom I meet in broadcloth have risen through their own efforts, and not because they were their father's children. President Buchanan was made our chief magistrate because he was himself, and not because of his father, or his ancestors, or because he was poorly or richly brought up. We put a premium on the proper exercise of every faculty, and guarantee to every man full freedom to better himself in any way he chooses, provided always he does not exercise it at the expense of the rights of other people. It is only those who refuse to avail themselves of their opportunities, and shamefully abuse them, that we condemn."

At other times, the vehemence of youth would frequently betray itself; and, if I had not been checked, I should probably have developed undue loquacity. Being of sanguine temper by nature, I was led through gushes of healthy rapture into excesses of speech; but he would turn on me, and gravely say that he was not accustomed to carry magnifiers with him; that, owing to his own sense of proportion, my figures gave him no true idea of the fact I wished to state, that my free use of unnecessary ciphers only created confusion in his mind. Sometimes he would assume a comical look of incredulity, which brought me to my senses very quickly, and made me retract what I had said, and repeat the statement with a more sacred regard for accuracy. "Just so," he would say; "if a thing is worth stating at all, it might as well be stated truly. A boy's fancy is very warm, I know; but, if once he acquires the habit of multiplying his figures, every fact will soon become no better than a fable."

Being an early riser himself, he insisted on my cultivating the habit of rising at dawn, but he also sent me to bed at an early hour. He lost no occasion to urge me to apply the morning hours to study; and, really, his anxiety that I should snatch the flying minutes appeared to be so great, that I was often infected with it as though they were something tangible, but so elusive that only a firm grasp would avail. If he saw me idly gazing on the shores, he would recall me, to ask if I had finished some chapter we had been discussing, or if I had found a different answer to his question than I had last given; and, if he detected an inclination in me to listen to the talk of passengers round the bar, he would ask if there were no books in the cabin, that I must needs hanker for the conversation of idlers. "All the babble of these topers, if boiled down," he would say, "would not give a drachm of useful knowledge. Greatness never sprang from such fruitless gossip. Those men were merely wasting time. From motives of selfishness, they, no doubt, would be glad to exchange trivial talk with anyone, big or little, who might come near them, but it was not to my interest to be in their company."

He would put his arm in mine, and lead me away to deliver himself of his thoughts on the glory of youth, painting it in such bright colours that, before long, I would be seized with a new idea of its beauty and value. It appeared to be only a brief holiday, which ought to be employed for the strengthening of muscles, gathering the flowers of knowledge, and culling the riper fruits of wisdom. Youth was, really, only the period for gaining strength of bone, to endure the weight put on it by manhood, and for acquiring that largeness of mind necessary to understand the ventures I should hereafter be compelled to take. To squander it among such fellows as congregated around bar-rooms and liquor-counters was as foolish as to open my veins to let out my life-blood. "Now is the time to prepare for the long voyage you are to take. You have seen the ships in the docks taking in their stores before leaving for the high sea where nothing can be bought. If the captains neglect their duties, the crews will starve. You are in the dock today; have you everything ready for your voyage? Are *all* your provisions aboard? If not, then, when you have hoisted your sails, it will be too late to think of them, and only good-luck can save you from misfortune"; and so on, until, through his forcible manner, earnestness, and copious similes, I returned to my studies with intense application.

The sight in the steamer saloons of crowds of excited gamblers was employed by him in exposition of his views on the various ways of acquiring wealth. Those piles of golden eagles that glittered on the table of the saloon would enrich none of the gamblers permanently. Money obtained by such methods always melted away. Wealth was made by industry and economy, and not by gambling or speculating. To know how to be frugal was the first step towards a fortune, the second was to practice frugality, and the third step was to know what to do with the money saved. It was every man's duty to put something aside each day, were it only a few cents. No man in America was paid such low wages that, if he were determined, he could not put away half of them. A man's best friend, after God, was himself; and, if he could not rely on himself, he could not rely on anybody else. His first duty was to himself, as he was bound to his own wants all his life, and must provide for them under every circumstance; if he neglected to provide for his own needs, he would always be unable to do anything towards the need of others. Then, as his custom was, he would proceed to apply these remarks to my case. I was to retain in my mind the possibility of being again homeless, and friendless, and adrift in the world, the world keeping itself to itself, and barring the door against me, as it did at Liverpool, New Orleans, and St. Louis. "The poor man is hated, even by his own neighbour; but the rich man has many friends," etc., etc.

An original method of instruction which he practised with me was to present me different circumstances, and ask me what I would do. These were generally difficult cases, wherein honesty, honour, and right-doing, were involved. No sooner had I answered, than he would press me with another view of it, wherein it appeared that his view was just as fair as the one I had; and he would so perplex me that I would feel quite foolish. For instance, a fellow-clerk of mine was secretly dishonest, but was attached to me in friendship. He made free with his employer's till, and one day was discovered by me alone. What would I do? I would dissuade him. But supposing, despite his promises to you, he was still continuing to abstract small sums: what then? I would accuse him of it, and say to him he was a thief. Supposing that, seeing you could give no positive proof of his theft, he denied it? Then he would be a liar, too, and there would be a quarrel. And what then? That is all. What of the employer? In what way? Is he not in question? Does he not pay you for looking after his interests? But I do look after his interests, in trying to prevent the theft. And yet, with all your care of his interests, the pilfering goes on, and nobody knows it but you. You think, then, that I ought to tell on him, and ruin him? Well, when you engaged with your employer, did you not make something of a bargain with him, that, for a certain wage you would make his interests your own, and keep him duly informed of all that was going on?

This is one example of the painstaking way in which would stir up my reasoning powers. When we walked through the streets, he would call my attention to the faces of the passers-by, and would question me as to what professions or trades they belonged to; and, when I replied that I could not guess them, he would tell me that my eyes were the lamps to my feet, and the guides to my understanding, and would show me that though I might not guess accurately each time, in many instances I might arrive at the truth, and that, whether wrong or right, the attempt to do so was an exercise of the intellect, and would greatly tend, in time, to sharpen my wits.

Moral resistance was a favourite subject with him. He said the practice of it gave vigour to the will, which required it much as the muscles. The will required to be strengthened to resist unholy desires and low passions, and was one of the best allies that conscience could have. Conscience was a good friend, and the more frequently I listened to it, the more ready it was with its good offices. Conscience was the sense of the soul; and, just as the senses of smell and taste guarded body from harm or annoyance, it guarded the spirit from evil. It was very tender and alert now, because I was yet at school and the influence of the Scriptures was strong in me; but, when neglected, it became dull and insensitive. Those, however, who paid heed to it grew to feel the sensation of its protective presence, and, upon the least suspicion of evil, it strenuously summoned the will to its aid, and thus it was that temptations were resisted.

Whether afloat or ashore, his manners were so open and genial, that one would think he courted acquaintance. Many people, led by this, were drawn to accost him; but no man knew better than he, how to relieve himself of undesirable people, and those who enjoyed his company were singularly like himself, in demeanour and conversation. It is from the character of his associates that I have obtained my most lasting impressions of Americans, and, whenever mentioned, these are the figures which always rise first in the mental view. "Punch's" "Jonathan"[10] I have never had the fortune to meet, though one who has travelled through two-thirds of the Union could scarcely have failed to meet him, if he were a common type. Among his kind, my adopted father was

10. "British officers contemptuously referred to the Americans as 'Cousin Jonathan,' a term meant to express disdain for their lack of military skill," notes Timothy Johnson. In the War of 1812, following American defeat at the Battle of Chrysler's Farm on November 11, 1813, a British officer observed, " 'This was Jonathan's debut on the open plain, . . . and I think, for the future, he will prefer his old mode of acting in the bush' " (Timothy D. Johnson, *Winfield Scott: The Quest for Military Glory* [Lawrence: University Press of Kansas, 1998], 39).

no mean figure. I once heard a man speak of him as "a man of a soft heart but a hard head," which I fancied had a sound of depreciation; but, later, I acknowledged it as just.

It was some six months or so after my adoption that I ventured to broach a subject of more than ordinary interest to me. In fact, it was my only remaining secret from him. It had been often on the tip of my tongue, but I had been restrained from mentioning it through fear of scorn. My ideas respecting the Deity I suspected were too peculiar to trust them to speech; and yet, if someone did not enlighten me, I should remain long in ignorance of the Divine character. True, certain coincidences made me secretly believe that God heard me; nevertheless, I burned to know from an authoritative source whether I was the victim of illusions, or whether the Being of my conceptions bore any resemblance to that of the learned and old I had met. I imagined God as a personality with human features, set in the midst of celestial Glory in the Heaven of Heavens; and, whenever I prayed, it was to Him thus framed that I directed my supplications. My father did not ridicule this idea as I feared he would, and I was much relieved to hear him ask how I had come to form such a fancy. This was difficult to express in words, but, at last, I managed to explain that, probably, it was from the verse which said that God had made man after His own image, and because clergymen always looked upward when in church.

I cannot give his own words, but this is the substance of my first intelligible lesson on this subject.

"God is a spirit, as you have often read. A spirit is a thing that cannot be seen with human eyes, because it has no figure or form. A man consists of body and spirit, or, as we call it, soul. The material part of him we can see and feel; but that which animates him, and governs his every thought, is invisible. When a person dies, we say his spirit has fled, or that his soul has departed to its Maker. The body is then as insensible as clay, and will soon corrupt, and become absorbed by the earth.

"We cannot see the air we breathe, nor the strong wind which wrecks ships, and blows houses down, yet we cannot live without air, and the effects of the winds are not disputed. We cannot see the earth move, and yet it is perpetually whirling through space. We cannot see that which draws the compass-needle to the Pole; yet we trust our ships to its guidance. No one saw the cause of that fever which killed so many people in New Orleans last summer, but we know it was in the air around the city. If you take a pinch of gunpowder and examine it, you cannot see the terrible force that is in it. So it is with the soul of man. While it is in him, you witness his lively emotions, and wonder at his intelligence and energy; but, when it has fled, it leaves behind only an inert and perishable thing, which must be buried quickly.

"Well! then, try and imagine the Universe subject to the same invisible but potent Intelligence, in the same way that man is subject to his. It is impossible for your eyes to see the thing itself; but, if you cannot see its effects, you must be blind. Day after day, year after year, since the beginning, that active and wonderful Intelligence has been keeping light and darkness, sun, moon, stars, and earth, each to their course in perfect order. Every living being on the earth today is a witness to its existence. The Intelligence that conceived this order and decreed that it should endure, that still sustains it, and will outlast every atom of creation, we describe under the term of God. It is a short word, but it signifies the Being that fills the Universe, and a portion of whom is in you and me.

"Now, what possible figure can you give of that Being that fills so large a space, and is everywhere? The sun is 95 millions of miles from us; imagine 95 millions of miles on the other side, yet the circle that would embrace those two points is but a small one compared to the whole of space. However far that space extends, the mighty Intelligence governs all. You are able to judge for yourself how inconceivable, for the mind of man, God is. The Bible says 'As the Heavens are higher than the earth, so are His ways higher than our ways.' God is simply indefinable, except as a spirit, but by that small fraction of Him which is in us, we are able to communicate with Him; for He so ordered it that we might be exalted the more we believe in Him."

"But how, then, am I to pray?" I asked, as my little mind tried to grasp this enormous space, and recoiled, baffled and helpless. "Must I only think, or utter the words, without regard to the object or way I direct them?"

"It seems to me our Saviour Himself has instructed us. He said, 'But thou, when thou prayest, enter into thy closet, and when thou hast shut thy door, pray to thy Father which is in secret; and thy Father, which seeth in secret, shall reward thee openly. Your Father knoweth what things ye have need of before ye ask Him.'

"Prayer is the expression of a wish of the heart, whether you speak aloud, or think it. You are a creature of God, destined to perform His design, be it great or little. Out of the limits of that design you cannot venture, therefore prayer will not avail you. Within the limits you will be wise to pray, in order that you may be guided aright. The understanding that He has seen fit to give you is equal to what you are destined to do. You may do it well, or ill; but that is left to your choice. How wide, or how narrow, those limits are, no one knows but Himself. Your existence may be compared to this: supposing I give you a sum of money which I know to be enough to take you to New Orleans and return here. If you spend that money faithfully and properly, it will suffice to bring you comfortably back; but, if you are foolish and waste it by the way, it may not even be enough to take you half-way on your journey. That is how I look upon our existence. God has furnished us with the necessary senses for the journey of life He has intended we should take. If we employ them wisely, they will take us safely to our journey's end; but if, through [our] perversion, we misuse them, it will be our own fault. By prayer our spirits communicate with God. We seek that wisdom, moral strength, courage, and patience to guide and sustain us on the way. The Father, who has all the time observed us, grants our wish, and the manner of it is past finding out; but the effect is like a feeling of restored health, or a burst of gladness. It is not necessary to make long or loud prayers: the whisper of a child is heard as well as the shout of a nation. It is purity of life, and sincerity of heart, that are wanted when you approach the Creator to implore His assistance. We must first render the service due to Him by our perfect conduct, before we seek favours from Him."

"But what does the verse 'So God created him in His image' mean, then?"

"If you still cling to the idea that the human form is a tiny likeness of the Almighty, you are more childish than I believed you to be. 'Image,' in the Bible sense, means simply a reflection. In our souls and intelligence we reflect, in a small way, God's own mightier spirit and intelligence, just as a small pocket mirror reflects the sun and the sky, or your eyes reflect the light."

Having had my doubts satisfied upon these essential points, there was only one thing more which I craved to know, and that was in regard to the Scriptures. Were they the words of God? If not, what was the Bible?

According to him, the Bible was the standard of the Christian faith, a fountain whence we derived our inspiration of piety and goodness, a proof that God interfered in human affairs, and a guide to salvation. He read from Timothy, " 'All scripture is given by inspiration of God, and is profitable for doctrine, for reproof, for correction, for instruction in righteousness: that the man of God may be perfect, thoroughly furnished unto all good works' "; and from Paul he quoted that " 'it was written for our learning, that we through patience and comfort might have hope.' "

"You are not," said he, "to pay too much attention to the set phrases, but to the matter and spirit of what is written, which are for the promotion of virtue and happiness. Many of the books have been written by men like ourselves, who lived between two thousand and four thousand years ago, and they used words peculiar to their own time. The mere texts or form of the words they used are not the exact words of God, but are simply the means of conveying the messages breathed into their understandings; and, naturally, they delivered them in the style of their period, and according to their ability, with such simplicity as would enable the common people to comprehend them. If I had to convey to you the proclamation of the President of the United States, I should have to write it more simply, and in a form that you would understand: so these Divine proclamations have been given to us by His chosen messengers, more faithfully than literally."

The above are a few of the intelligent ideas which I obtained from my father, and for which I have been as grateful as for his unusual goodness in other respects. Probably, many a sermon which I had heard had contained them in a diluted form; but they had not been adapted to my understanding, and his clear exposition of these subjects was an immense relief to me. It was a fortunate thing for me that my foggy beliefs, and vague notions, in regard to such high matters, could be laid open with all trust and confidence before one so qualified and tender, before they became too established in my mind, otherwise, as my own intelligence ripened, I might have drifted into atheistical indifference. The substance of my father's sayings, which I have always remembered, illustrate the bent of his mind. I carefully copied them into a beautiful memorandum-book of which he made me a present, New Year's Day, 1860, and which I was so proud of that, during the first few days, I had filled more than half of it with the best words of my father.

It must not be supposed that I was at all times deserving of his solicitude, or equal to his expectations. I was one who could not always do
the right and proper thing, for I was often erring and perverse, and at
various times must have tried him sorely. My temper was quick, which,
with an excess of false pride, inspired me to the verge of rebellion. A
sense of decency prevented me from any overt act of defiance, but the
spirit was not less fierce because I imposed the needful restraint on it.
Outwardly, I might be tranquil enough, but my smothered resentment
was as wicked and unjustifiable as if I had openly defied him. A choleric
disposition on his part would have been as a flame to my nature, and
the result might have been guessed. Happily for me, he was consistently
considerate, and declined to notice too closely the flushed face, and the
angry sparkles of the eye, which betokened revolt. An occasional blood-
letting might perhaps have been beneficial to me; but he had discovered
other methods, just as efficacious, for reducing me to a state of reason,
and never once had recourse to threats. My fits of sullenness had been
probably provoked by an unexpected sharpness of tone, or a denial of
some liberty, or graver censure than I thought I deserved. Constrained
to silence by the magnitude and character of my obligations to him, I,
of course, magnified my grievances; and, the longer reconciliation was
deferred, the larger these seemed. Before this dangerous mood sought
vent, some look, a word, some secret transmission of sympathy occurred, and, in an instant, the evil humour vanished; for weeks afterwards, I would endeavour to atone for my churlish behaviour by a
contrite submissiveness which was capable of undergoing any penance.

"I do not punish you," he said, "because I want you to remember
that you are a little man, and the only difference between us is that I am
an older man. If I were in the habit of striking you, you would run away
from me, or it would be noticeable in you by a slinking gait, or a sly eye,
or a sullen disposition, or a defiant look, or you would become broken-
spirited; all this I do not want you to be—I wish for your filial regard,
and your respect, which I would not deserve if I terrified. Misery and
suffering would wreck your temper, while kindness and reason will
bring out the best qualities of your nature; for you, as well as every child
that is born, possess something that is good, and it is the sunshine of
tenderness that makes it grow."

To one who considers that neither the closest ties of relationship,
nor the highest claims of affection, are sufficient to preserve the rebel-

lious spirit in an angelic temper for a long time, this boyish inconsistency and perverseness will be no surprise; but I was sensible that it was only owing to his patience that it did not receive the condign punishment it deserved. This, in itself, was an education; for I learned, after several experiences, not to disturb myself too seriously because of a temporary change in his manner or mood, and to accept it rather as being due to some cross in business, or physical condition, than to any offence in me, and so the customary cordiality was soon restored.

If I could only have made similar allowances earlier, and with other persons in later life, I should have had much less unhappiness to bewail; but, in his case, the necessity of doing so was impressed on me by my intimate knowledge of his fatherliness, and affectionate considerateness, and by the constant sense that I owed him unreserved submission.

4

Adrift Again

My education did not consist solely of his discussions upon books, morality, and religion, but it embraced a countless variety of topics suggested by our travels. By [my father's] method of teaching, no passive reception of facts was possible, and the stimulus to intellect was given by being urged to observe, sift, and examine every article of conversation. I absorbed considerable practical knowledge during this period. His level-headedness, which I was prone to regard at that time as the height of worldly wisdom, and his intense realness, aided greatly to clarify my ideas upon many things, and was excellently adapted to form a sound judgement. He could be as genial as a glad boy on his summer holiday, lofty as a preacher, frank as a brother; but righteously austere, hilariously familiar and jocose, yet sublime, according to occasion. The candour and good faith with which he spoke, the expansive benevolence, and the large amount of sympathy he always showed when I sought his advice, or exposed my doubts or fears, were the very qualities which were best calculated to ensure my affection, extract my shy confidences, and cultivate in me a fearless openness. With the exception of those fits of sullen resentment to which I was now and then subject, like other human whelps, my life with him was one unbroken period of pleasantness, and, so far as I required and knew, every condition of a Paradise was present, in the unfretting, fair, and healthful existence which I led.

I sometimes imagine that he must have discerned something attractive in me, though I myself was unconscious of the cause. If I review my appearance at that time, I can find nothing to admire. I was naturally shy, silent, short of figure, poorly clad, uninteresting, and yet he chose me, from the first moment he saw me, to be an object of his charity. I endeavoured to be, as the phrase is, good and grateful; but, as I have reason to remember, I was by no means perfect in my endeavours. I think zeal, good-will, docility, were my only commendable traits; but they strike me now as being insufficient to account for my undeniable good fortune.

I can only remember one noticeable incident, outside of the common, in connection with this period, and that occurred in the middle of 1860. We were passengers on the steamer *Little Rock*, as she was returning, laden with cotton, down the Washita.[1] My father had been paid money due to him for goods by a merchant near Fairview, and, through neglect, or some other reason, had deferred entrusting it to the purser longer than he ought. We were approaching near Sicily Island, when, in the gloom caused by the mountain-pile of cotton bales, I observed a man lingering rather suspiciously near our cabin-door. At first, I took him for one of the stewards; but, on observing him more particularly, his conduct, I thought, suggested some nefarious design. My father had retired, and, according to custom, I ought to have been abed; but the unusual freight of cotton the boat carried had kept me in a state of suppressed excitement. Being light and active, I ensconced myself in a dark gap between two tiers of bales, and waited patiently. After a little time the man put his ear to our door, and presently opened it, and entered our cabin. In a few minutes, I heard my father's voice ask, "Who is there?" and, immediately, sounds of a struggle were heard. Upon this I bounded in, and found the stranger wrestling with my father, and one of the two seemed to be choking. Upon seeing me, the intruder turned rapidly towards me. I saw the flash as of steel, and something struck me between my arm and left breast in my overcoat, and a piece of metal tinkled on the floor. Then, with a deep curse, I was flung aside, and the man fled along the guards. We instantly raised a cry of "Thieves!" which brought crowds of stewards and passengers to us, carrying lights. These revealed an open portmanteau, with rumpled contents, and the half of a carving-knife blade on the floor. On examining my coat it was seen that it had a cut as far as the canvas stiffening. All these evidences tended to prove that a daring attempt at robbery had been made, and, it

1. Flowing parallel to the Arkansas River, the Washita (Ouachita) connected Hot Springs, Rockport, Arkadelphia, and Camden.

was suspected, by someone connected with the boat. The chief steward mustered the waiters, but they all answered to their names. He next counted the carving-knives, and, according to him, one was missing. The incident caused quite a commotion for the time, but the culprit was never discovered.

Beyond this incident, we were singularly free from mishaps, and exciting episodes, upon waters that had been the scene of many a calamity; and yet, when I chanced to find myself among a group of passengers, I frequently heard terrible recitals of experiences at boiler-explosions, and shipwrecks, and other events hazardous to life.[2] We had often been fellow-passengers with gamblers, some of whom were wrought into fury by their losses at cards; but, whether it was owing to my good or evil fortune, I never happened to be present when the issue was left to the arbitrament of revolver and bowie-knife, as there were plenty of peace-makers always ready to interfere at the critical moment.

In September of 1860, we met a tall and spruce gentleman, of the name of Major Ingham, on board a steamer bound to New Orleans.[3] From what I gathered, he was a South Carolinian by birth, but, some few years since, had removed to Saline County, Arkansas, and had established a plantation not far from Warren.[4] My father and he had an abundant amount of small-talk together relating to acquaintances and

2. It is difficult for those living in the early twenty-first century to imagine the dangers of river travel in the 1850 to 1870 era. Fires, explosions, wrecks seemed the rule. For a spectator's glimpse of one of these sudden disasters, occurring nearby in 1859, see Nathaniel C. Hughes, Jr., *The Life and Wars of Gideon J. Pillow* (Chapel Hill: University of North Carolina Press, 1993), 152.

3. HMS's chronology seems to break down at this point. The date of the census of Auburn, Arkansas, is August 22, 1860, which means that HMS probably had begun work in Altshur's store, and may have been there for some months (see n. 8 in chapter 3).

4. An investigation of the 1860 census for Saline County failed to produce Major Ingham or his friend Mr. Waring (mentioned later in this chapter), but just to the southeast, in Jefferson County (Washington township), lived physician-farmer A. H. Ingram and his elder brother B. F., both sons of John M. Ingram. The family had emigrated by wagon train to Arkansas from North Carolina in 1856. A. H. Ingram had been born in Mecklenburg, North Carolina, and attended Davidson College. He graduated from the Medical College of Charleston in 1845 and practiced medicine in Anson County, North Carolina, until moving to Arkansas. In time he would acquire large tracts of land and is shown in 1880 with four thousand acres. The Major Ingham with whom HHS conversed may have been A. H. Ingram or his father, John M. (1860 Census of Jefferson County, Arkansas, HH 40, HH 47; Weston Goodspeed, *Biographical and Historical Memoirs of Central Arkansas* [Chicago: Goodspeed Publishing, 1889], 181).

localities, which occupied their leisure during the voyage. The Major also ingratiated himself with me, and, through his description of the forests of pine and oak, and accounts of the wild animals, such as cata-mounts, bears, and deer, in his region, I became warmly attached to him. Before reaching New Orleans, we had become so intimate that he extended an invitation to me to spend a month with him on his Arkan-sas plantation; and, on referring him to father, I found that he was not so averse to the proposal as I feared he would be. The subject was de-ferred for further consideration in the city.

After about a fortnight's stay at the St. Charles Hotel, my father was made anxious by a letter from Havana from his brother, and he resolved to go and see him. He then disclosed to me that after much mental dis-cussion he had concluded that Major Ingham's invitation had assisted greatly in smoothing matters. For some time he had been debating as to how it would be best to take the first step for establishing my future. He had been much struck with the opportunities for doing a good busi-ness in a country store, at some place below Pine Bluff on the Arkansas. There were a large number of planters settled there, and a general sup-ply store such as he had fancied for their convenience could not fail to be a success. Major Ingham's plantation was situated about forty miles back of the Arkansas River, and, at Cypress Bend, there was a friend of his who, upon a letter from him, would take me in to teach me the de-tails of a country merchant's business. Here was an opportunity of ap-proaching his project in a methodical way without loss of time. His brother's illness at Havana had caused some confusion in his affairs, and it was necessary for him to cross the Gulf and set things in order.[5] Meantime, I had a safe escort to within a day's drive of the merchant's store, to which, after being tired of the plantation, I was to go to be grounded in the minutiae of a retail store; and in a few months he would have wound up his commission business, and be able to avail himself of my local knowledge, and proceed to choose the best locality.

5. McLynn believes "a decisive rupture took place" between HMS and HHS around this time: "The causes of the quarrel remain obscure, but the result was that Stanley sen-ior sent his refractory protégé to work on a friend's plantation in Arkansas." Bierman concurs but thinks that HMS "wanted more than a benefactor; he wanted a family," so HHS rid himself of HMS. "The young Rowlands' rage and hurt at this rejection would certainly account for his symbolic murder of the older man" (McLynn, *Stanley*, 37–38; Bierman, *Dark Safari*, 28).

I saw no objection to any of his arrangements, as they rather coincided with my secret ambitions, which had been fostered by many previous allusions to such a scheme as had been now explained. The suddenness of the parting was somewhat of a drawback to the beauty of the project; but, as accident was the cause, and his absence was to be only for a few months, during which we could often correspond, I became inclined, with the sanguineness of my nature, to anticipate much enjoyment from the novelty of the situation. In my highly-coloured fancy, I saw illimitable pine-woods, infested by Indians, and by wild-cats, and other savage felines; and the fact that I was about to prepare myself to be a dealer in merchandise, preliminary to a permanent establishment, appeared such an enchanting prospect that I felt no disposition to peer into sober realities. Could we have foreseen, however, that this parting so calmly proposed and so trustfully accepted, was to be for ever, both of us would have shrunk from the thought of it; but, unknown to ourselves, we had arrived at the parting of the ways, and though we both sincerely hoped the ways would meet, we were gliding along steep planes which would presently precipitate us into the wide gulf of separation.

From the moment it was agreed to part for a while, my father lost no opportunity to fill me with practical counsel, which, had my memory been a knapsack, I could have extracted at will for consolation and guidance. Unfortunately, for some things my memory was like a sieve: it retained the larger rules, but dropped the lesser ones; it preserved certain principles that had an affinity with my nature, but the multitude of minor ones that he had attempted to graft on my nature fell away, one by one. I was to be industrious, orderly, honourable, and steady, patient, and obliging. But something of these I would naturally have shown under any circumstances; but contact with real life discovers that these virtues are insufficient to keep us serene and immaculate, that the spirit of youth requires its sensibilities to be disciplined in many ways before it endures with sweetness and patience the spurns, and gibes, and mocks, of a rude world. It frequently meets conditions wherein nothing will avail but force, of a most strenuous kind.

When the hour came for my father's departure, Major Ingham and I accompanied him on board the Havana steamer. The last parting occurred in the state-room. At that moment, there was a wild fluttering of the heart; and something like an ugly cloud of presentiments, vague shadows of unknown evils to come, which started strong doubts of the wisdom of parting, came over me all at once. But, as usual, when clear expression was most needed, I was too tongue-tied for much speech, so many ideas thronged for utterance, and I turned away as though stricken dumb. Half an hour later, the steamer was only discernible by its trail of smoke.

After he had gone, the flood-gates were opened, the feelings relieved themselves by torrents of words, and my loss and loneliness pressed hard upon the senses. Much as I had valued him, it needed this time of anguish to reveal fully what he had been to me. Then, pang after pang of poignant contrition pierced me through and through. I was dissatis-fied with the sum of my conduct, with his own professions that I had been to him what he had hoped and wished. If he had but returned there and then, with the clear light that fell on my deficiencies now, how I should have striven to satisfy my own exact ideas of what was due to him! This little absence, with its unutterable remorse, had been more efficacious in showing me my own inwardness than all his unselfish gen-erosity.

Nearly five and thirty years have passed since, and I have not experi-enced such wretchedness as I did that night following his departure. A very little more, and I think it would have exceeded the heart's power to bear. My emotions were much more distressing than anyone could have judged from my appearance. I caught a view of myself in a mirror, and my face struck me as exhibiting an astonishing contrast to the huge disorder beneath it. For the first time, I understood the sharpness of the pang which pierces the soul when a loved one lies with folded hands, icy cold, in the sleep of Death. I vexed myself with asking, Had my con-duct been as perfect as I then wished it had been? Had I failed in aught? Had I esteemed him as he deserved? Then a craving wish to hear him speak but one word of consolation, to utter one word of blessing, made me address him as though he might hear; but no answer came, and I experienced a shiver of sadness and wished that I could die.

I have often looked back upon the boy who sat like a stone in his father's chair for hours, revolving with fixed eyes and unmoved face all that this parting seemed to him to mean. Up to a certain point he traced minutely all its details, went over every word and little act, and then a great blank wall met him, into which he strove and strove again to pene-trate, and being baffled, resumed his mental rehearsals.

Before Major Ingham turned his steps homeward, I received a letter from my father duly announcing his arrival at the island of Cuba. After describing the passage across the Gulf, he went on to say that the more he thought of his plans, the more he was inclined to regard the Major's invitation as a happy incident in his programme. He had often pondered over the best means of starting me in a business for which I had decided bent, and he had been sounding several country merchants with a view of giving me a preliminary training, but he had constantly deferred a decision in the hope of finding something that more nearly suited his ideas. Now, however, it all seemed clear. He had always fancied the Arkansas River, as it had a richer back country than any other, and, by means of the steamers and its superior navigation, was in direct communication with the cities on the Mississippi. There were many professions and trades for which I was fit, but he thought that I was more partial to a mercantile career, and he was glad of it. He went on to say that I had made a wonderful advance during the last year with him, but it was on the next few years that my future depended. For tiding over them successfully, I had only to hold fast to my principles, and be fearless in all manly things; to persevere and win.

The letter seemed to be his very self, full of practical sense. I felt enriched by its possession. It was a novelty to have a letter of my own, sent from such a distance. I read it over and over, and found new meanings and greater solace each time. The signature attracted my attention with its peculiar whip, or flourish, below; and in my reply, which covered many pages, I annexed that whip and ended my first epistle with it; and, ever since, no signature of mine has been complete without it.

Soon after, Major Ingham started on his return home in a stern-wheeler bound for the Washita and Saline Rivers. The Washita, next to the Arkansas, is the most important river which passes through the state of Arkansas—pronounced "Arkansaw." The Saline is one of its feeders, and has a navigable course of only about one hundred and twenty-five miles. The Washita in its turn empties into the Red River, and the latter into the Mississippi.

On, or about, the seventh day from New Orleans, the steamer entered the Saline, and a few miles above Long View we landed on the right bank, and, mounting into a well-worn buggy, were driven a few miles inland to Ingham's plantation.

I am as unaware of the real status of my host among his neighbours, as I am of the size of his domain. It then appeared in my eyes immense, but was mostly a pine forest, in the midst of which some few score of black men had cleared a large space for planting. The house was of solid pine logs, roughly squared, and but slightly stained by weather, and neatly chinked without with plaster, and lined within with planed boards, new and unpainted—it had an air of domestic comfort.

My welcome from Mrs. Ingham left nothing to be desired. The slaves of the house thronged in her train, and curtsied and bobbed, with every token of genuine gladness, to the "Massa," as they called him, and then were good enough to include me in their bountiful joy. The supper which had been got ready was something of a banquet, for it was to celebrate the return of the planter, and was calculated to prove to him that, though New Orleans hotels might furnish more variety, home, after all, had its attractions in pure, clean, well-cooked viands. When the hearth-logs began to crackle, and the fire-light danced joyfully on the family circle, I began to feel the influence of the charm, and was ready to view my stay in the western woods with interest and content.

But there was one person in the family that caused a doubt in my mind, and that was the overseer. He joined us after supper, and, almost immediately, I contracted a dislike for him. His vulgarity and coarseness revived recollections of levee men. His garb was offensive; the pantaloons stuffed into his boots, the big hat, the slouch of his carriage, his rough boisterousness, were all objectionable, and more than all his accents and the manner of his half-patronising familiarity. I set him down at once as one of those men who haunt liquor-saloons, and are proud to claim acquaintance with bar-tenders. Something in me, perhaps my offishness, may probably have struck him with equal repulsion. Under pretence of weariness I sought my bed, for the circle had lost its charm.

The next day the diet was not so sumptuous. The breakfast at seven, the dinner at noon, and the supper at six, consisted of pretty much the same kind of dishes, except that there was good coffee at the first meal, and plenty of good milk for the last. The rest mainly consisted of boiled, or fried, pork and beans, and corn scones. The pork had an excess of fat over the lean, and was followed by a plate full of mush and molasses. I was never very particular as to my diet, but as day after day followed, the want of variety caused it to pall on the palate. Provided other things had not tended to make me critical, I might have gratefully endured it, but what affected me principally were the encomiums lavished upon this style of cookery by the overseer, who, whether with the view of currying favour with Mrs. Ingham, or to exasperate my suppressed squeamishness, would bawl out, "I guess you can't beat this, howsumdever you crack up New Or-lee-ans. Give me a raal western pot-luck, to your darned fixin's in them 'ar Mississippi towns."

With such society and fare, I could not help feeling depressed, but the tall pine forest, with its mysterious lights and shades, had its compensations. As, in process of time, the planter intended to extend his clearing and raise more cotton, every tree felled assisted in widening the cultivable land. On learning this, I asked and obtained permission to cut down as many trees as I liked, and, like a ruthless youth with latent destructive propensities, I found an extraordinary pleasure in laying low with a keen axe the broad pines. I welcomed with a savage delight the apparent agony, the portentous shiver which ran from root to topmost plume, the thunderous fall, and the wild recoil of its neighbours, as it rebounded and quivered before it lay its still length. After about a score of the pine monarchs had been levelled, the negroes at work presented new features of interest. On the outskirts of the clearing they were chopping up timber into portable or rollable logs, some were "toting" logs to the blazing piles, others rolled them hand over hand to the fires, and each gang chanted heartily as it toiled. As they appeared to enjoy it, I became infected with their spirit and assisted at the log-rolling, or lent a hand at the toting, and championed my side against the opposite. I waxed so enthusiastic over this manly work, which demanded the exertion of every ounce of muscle, that it is a marvel I did not suffer from the strain; its fierce joy was more to my taste than felling timber by myself. The atmosphere, laden with the scent of burning resin, the roaring fires, the dance of the lively flames, the excitement of the gangs while holding on, with grim resolve and in honour bound, to the bearing-spikes, had a real fascination for me. For a week, I rose with the darkies at the sound of the overseer's horn, greeted the revivifying sunrise with anticipating spirits, sat down to breakfast with a glow which made the Major and his wife cheerier, and then strode off to join in the war against the pines with a springy pace.

How long this toil would have retained its sportive aspect for me I know not, but I owed it to the overseer that I ceased to love it. He was a compound of a Legree and Nelson, with an admixture of mannerism peculiarly his own.[6] It was his duty to oversee all the gangs, the hoers, wood-cutters, fire-attendants, log-rollers, and toters. When he approached the gang with which I worked, the men became subdued, and stopped their innocent chaff and play. He had two favourite songs: one was about his "dear Lucindah," and the other about the "chill winds of December," which he hummed in a nasal tone when within speaking distance of me, while the cracks of his "black snake" whip kept time. But, as he sauntered away to other parts, I felt he was often restive at my presence, for it imposed a certain restraint on his nature. One day, however, he was in a worse humour than usual. His face was longer, and malice gleamed in his eyes. When he reached us we missed the usual tunes. He cried out his commands with a more imperious note. A young fellow named Jim was the first victim of his ire, and, as he was carrying a heavy log with myself and others, he could not answer him so politely as he expected. He flicked at his naked shoulders with his whip, and the lash, flying unexpectedly near me, caused us both to drop our spikes. Unassisted by us, the weight of the log was too great for the others, and it fell to the ground crushing the foot of one of them. Meantime, furious at the indignity, I had engaged him in a wordy contest: hot words, even threats, were exchanged, and had it not been for the cries of the wounded man who was held fast by the log, we should probably have fought. The end of it was, I retired from the field, burning with indignation, and disgusted with his abominable brutality.

I sought Major Ingham, whom I found reclining his length in an easy-chair on the verandah. Not hearing the righteous condemnation I had hoped he would express, and surprised at his want of feeling, I hotly protested against the cruelty of the overseer in attacking a man while all his strength was needed to preserve others from peril, and declaimed against him for using a whip in proximity to my ears, which made the Major smile compassionately at my inexperience in such matters. This was too much for my patience, and I then and there announced my intention to seek the hospitality of Mr. Waring, his neighbour, as I could not be any longer the guest of a man who received my complaint so unsympathetically. On hearing me say this, Mrs. Ingham came out of the house, and expressed so much concern at this sudden rupture of our

6. DTS's note: "The cruel slave-driver, in *Uncle Tom's Cabin*, comparable with Nelson, bully of the *Windermere*" (Stanley, *Autobiography*, 148n).

relations that I regretted having been so hasty, and the Major tried to explain how planters were compelled to leave fieldwork in charge of their overseer; but it was too late. Words had been uttered which left a blister in the mind, personal dignity had been grossly wounded, the Major had not the art of salving sores of this kind, and I doggedly clung to my first intentions. In another quarter of an hour I had left the plantation with a small bundle of letters and papers, and was trudging through the woods to Mr. Waring's plantation.

We have all our sudden likes and dislikes. The first view of the comfortable homeliness of Mr. Waring's house gave me an impression of family felicity, and when the old man with several smiling members of his family came to the door, it appeared to me as if it revived a picture I had seen somewhere in Wales, and all my heart went out to those who were in the house.

Strange to say, in proportion to the period spent at Major Ingham's, I possess a more vivid recollection of the night I passed at Mr. Waring's, and my thoughts have more often reverted to the more ancient house and its snugness and pleasant details, than to the other. As I did not mention anything about the causes of my departure from his neighbour's plantation, it was tacitly understood that I was only resting for the night, previous to resuming my journey next morning, and they did not press me to stay. I begged, however, Mr. Waring to do me the favour to send a buggy for my trunk the next morning. When it arrived, I repacked it; and, leaving it in his charge, I set off on a tramp across country to the Arkansas, rejecting many an offer of aid up to the last minute.

The road wound up and down pine-clothed hills, and, being a sandy loam, was dry and tolerably smooth. In the hollows I generally found a stream where I quenched my thirst, but I remember to have travelled a considerable distance for a young pedestrian without meeting any water, and to have reflected a little upon what the pains of dying from thirst would be like. I rested at a small farm-house that night; and, next morning, at an early hour, was once more footing it bravely, more elated, perhaps, than my condition justified. I regarded myself as being upon a fine adventure, the narration of which would surprise my father. My eyes travelled through far-reaching colonnades of tapering pine and flourishing oak, and for a great part of the time I lost consciousness of my circumstances, while my mind was absorbed in interminable imaginings of impossible discoveries and incidents. I saw myself the hero of many a thrilling surprise, and looked dreamily through the shades, as though in some places like them I would meet the preying beasts whom it would be my fortune to strike dead with my staff. But, invariably, on being brought to a proper sense of the scenes, and my real condition, I recognized how helpless I was against a snarling catamount, or couchant panther; I was devoutly thankful that Arkansas was so civilised that my courage was in no fear of being tested.

Just at dusk I reached the Arkansas River at Cypress Bend, having travelled about forty miles across country, without having met a single adventure.[7]

Mr. Altschul's store, at which I was to devote myself to acquiring the arts and details of a country merchant's business, was situated about fifty miles S.E. of Little Rock, and half-way between Richmond [Richland] and South Bend.[8] I found no difficulty at all in entering the establishment, for I had no sooner introduced myself than I was accepted by his family with all cordiality. The store was, in reality, a country house of business. It stood isolated in a small clearing in the midst of Cypress Grove, and was removed from the dwelling-house of the family by a quarter of a mile. It was a long one-storied building of solid logs, divided into four apartments, three of which contained all manner of things that ironmongers, gunners, grocers, drapers, stationers, are supposed to sell; the fourth room, at the back, was used as an office during the day and as a bedroom at night, by the clerks in charge. I commenced

7. The area in which HMS found himself was rich in folklore. Here John James Audubon, "the bird portrayer," had stayed and explored, as had Timothy Flint, geographer, minister, and later territorial governor. Indeed, the first territorial capitol was at nearby Arkansas Post, and close to the mouth of the White River, at Montgomery Point, hid Murrell, the "satanic outlaw preacher and slave-runner and his gang" (T. L. Hodges, "Possibilities for the Archaeologist and Historian in Eastern Arkansas," *Arkansas Historical Quarterly* 2 [June 1943]: 155).

8. The 1860 Census of Arkansas County, Arkansas, HH 599, Douglas township, South Bend post office, lists:

Isaac Altschur, 36, male, merchant $10,000 (pers. property)	born Germany
Terace Altschur, 23, female, housekeeper	born Germany
Joseph Altshur, 6, male	born Arkansas
Infant Altshur, 7/12	born Arkansas
William H. Stanley, 17, male, clerking in store	born Arkansas

my duties in November, 1860, being warmly hailed as a fellow-clerk by Mr. Cronin, the salesman, and Mr. Waldron, the assistant-salesman.[9]

Cronin was an Irishman from New York, about thirty years old; the assistant was the son of a small planter in the vicinity. The first was a character for whom I had a pitying fondness. One-half of him was excellent, all brightness, cleverness, and sociability, the other half, perhaps the worse, was steeped in whiskey. He was my Alphabet of the race of topers. I have never been able to be wrathful with his kind, they are such miracles of absurdity! Here and there one may meet a malignant, but they are mostly too stupid to be hated. Cronin knew his duties thoroughly. He was assiduous, obliging, and artful beyond anything with the ladies. He won their confidences, divined their preferences, and, with the most provoking assurance, laid the identical piece of goods they wanted before them, and made them buy it. It was a treat to observe the cordial, and yet deferent, air with which he listened to their wishes, the deft assistance he gave to their expression, his bland assents, the officious haste and zeal he exhibited in attending on them, and the ruthless way he piled the counters with goods for their inspection. Sometimes I suspected he was maliciously making work for me, for, being the junior, I had to refold the goods, and restore them to their places; but, in justice to him, I must say he nobly assisted in the re-arrangement. Cronin was a born salesman, and I have never met his equal since.

The poorer class of women he dazzled by his eloquent commendations, his elaborate courtesy, and the way he made them conceited with their own superior knowledge of what was genuine and rich. If the woman was a coloured person, he was benevolent and slightly familiar. His small grey eyes twinkled with humour, as he whispered friendly advice as to the quality of the goods, and besieged her with such attentions that the poor thing was compelled to buy.

With the planters, who were of varying moods, Mr. Cronin bore himself with such rare good-humour and tact, that one found a pleasure in watching the stern lips relax, and the benignant look coming to their

9. Cronin does not appear in the 1860 Census of Arkansas County, Arkansas, but one finds listed in Douglas township, HH 608, a James Waldren, thirty-one years old, farmer, born in Tennessee.

gloomy eyes. He would go forward to meet them, as they stepped across the threshold, with hearty abandon and joviality, put fervour into his hand-shakes, sincerity into his greeting, and welcome into his every act. He anxiously enquired after their healths, condoled with them in their fevers, sympathised with them in their troubles about their cotton-crops, and soon found excuse to draw them to the liquor apartment, where he made them taste Mr. Altschul's latest importations.

According to Mr. Cronin, the "cobwebs" were cleared by the preliminary drink, and it enabled both salesman and buyer to take a cheerier view of things, and to banish thoughts that would impede business. Naturally, the planters cared little for cotton-prints or jaconets, though they often carried daintily-pencilled commissions from the ladies at home, which Mr. Cronin satisfactorily executed at once, on the plea that the ladies must be served first; but when these were disposed of,— always with reverent regard for the fair sex—Mr. Cronin flung off his tenderness and became the genial salesman again. Had the gentleman seen the new Californian saddles, or the latest thing in rifles, shot-guns that would kill duck at ninety yards? Those who heard him expatiate upon the merits of fire-arms wondered at the earnestness he threw into his language, and at the minute knowledge he seemed to possess of the properties of each article. Or the subject was saddles. I heard with amazement about the comparative excellencies of the Californian, English, and cavalry article,[10] and thought his remarks ought to be printed. In this way, with regard to rifles, I soon got to know all about the merits of the Ballard, Sharp, Jocelyn rifles,[11] their special mechanisms, trajec-

10. The Californian saddle appears to have been "popular for riding 'bad horses,' " a saddle with a "slightly swelled fork with a high steel horn bolted to it." The English saddle featured the "balanced seat," which tended to throw the rider forward and almost forced the rider to sit tall and upright. The military saddle generally meant the McClellan saddle, borrowed by George B. McClellan from the Hungarian hussars. It was easy on the horse and thought to be "hard on the rider," although acknowledged fine for long distances (Russel H. Beatie, *Saddles* [Norman: University of Oklahoma Press, 1981], 59, 67, 78, 144, 301).

11. The Ballard rifle, manufactured by C. H. Ballard of Fall River, Massachusetts, was probably not yet in production. Its first patent came November 5, 1861. Christian Sharp's highly popular breechloading percussion rifle had been developed in the late 1840s at Sharp's Rifle Manufacturing Company, Hartford, Connecticut, and at C. Sharp and Company, Philadelphia. Benjamin F. Joslyn of Worcester, Massachusetts, developed the .54 caliber Joslyn breechloading percussion carbine in the late 1850s (Arcadi Gluckman, *United States Muskets, Rifles, and Carbines* [Buffalo: Otto Ulbrich, 1948], 266–67, 301, 308–309, 409).

tory, penetration, and range. If I alluded to the revolvers, his face glowed with a child's rapture as he dilated upon the superiority of the Tranter[12] over the Colt, or the old-fashioned "pepper-box"[13]; but, when he took up a beautiful Smith and Wesson,[14] he became intoxicated with his own bewildering fluency, and his gestures were those of an oratorical expert. Then some other excuse would be found for adjourning to the liquor room, where he continued to hold forth with his charming persuasiveness, until he succeeded in effecting a sale of something.

Mr. Cronin was indeed an artist, but Mr. Altschul did not appreciate him as his genius deserved. The proprietor laid too much stress upon his propensity to drink, which was certainly incurable, and too little upon the profits accruing to him through his agency. He also suspected him of gross familiarities with female slaves, which, in Mr. Altschul's eyes, were unpardonable. Therefore, though he was invaluable to me as a model salesman, poor Cronin was obliged to leave after a while.[15]

Waldron in a short time found counter-work too irksome and frivolous for his nature, and he also left; then two young men, very proud and high-stomached, and not over-genial to customers, were engaged instead.

But by this time I had become sufficiently acquainted with the tone of the planter community to be able to do very well, with a few instructions from Mr. Altschul. I had learned that in the fat cypress lands there was a humanity which was very different from that complaisant kind dwelling in cities. It had been drawn from many States, especially from the South. The Douglasses were from Virginia, the Crawfords from "Old Geor-

---

12. The English gunsmith William Tranter held many English patents, and his pistols were highly regarded. The "Tranters" were known for their double-trigger locking mechanisms. His pepperbox was also noted for its locking system. This is probably an anachronism by HMS, for Tranter and his weapons became more famous after 1865 (see A. W. F. Taylerson, R. A. N. Andrews, and J. Frith, *The Revolver, 1818–1865* [New York: Crown Publishers, 1968], 272–90; Frederick Wilkinson, *Small Arms* [New York: Hawthorn Books, 1965]).

13. The pepperbox (a multi-barreled pistol) was a concept dating back to the sixteenth century. There seemed to be an infinite variety of styles (see Taylerson, Andrews, and Frith, *The Revolver*, 124ff.).

14. For information about the highly regarded Smith and Wesson breechloader, see Taylerson, Andrews, and Frith, *The Revolver*, 263, 333–34.

15. "Poor Cronin," with his charm and susceptibilities, seemed to confirm HMS's bias against the Irish Roman Catholics, learned, he maintained, in the "repulsiveness" of Irish Square at St. Asaph (Stanley, *Autobiography*, 21).

gia," the Joneses and Smiths from Tennessee, the Gorees from Alabama.[16] The poorer sort were from the Carolinas, Mississippi, Missouri, and Tennessee, the professional men and white employers from a wider area—which included Europe. Several of the richer men owned domains of from six to ten square miles. They lived like princelings, were owners of hundreds of slaves over whom they were absolute except as to life or limb, and all their environments catered to their egotism. Though genially sociable to each other, to landless people like myself they conducted themselves as though they were under no obligations. Such manners as they exhibited were not so much due to neighbourly good-feeling as to their dislike of consequences which might result from a wanton offishness. When they emerged from their respective territories to the common view, their bearing seemed to say that they yielded to us every privilege belonging to free whites, but reserved to themselves the right to behave as they deemed fitting to their state, and of airing any peculiarity unquestioned, and unremarked by the commonalty. They were as exclusive as the proud county families of Wales.

It may easily be seen, then, what a sight our store presented when about a dozen magnates of this kind, fresh from their cotton principalities, and armed, cap-à-pie,[17] each in his own peculiar dress, assembled

---

16. HMS's memory is quite accurate as seen from the following 1860 Census entries, Arkansas County, Arkansas, South Bend post office:

> Household 604: William H. Crawford 46m 10,000/28,000 bn Ga. and wife Caroline and 5 children, farmer.

> Household 639 (Auburn P.O.):

Goree, James L.	41m	farmer 78,000/87,900	born Ala.
, Mary E.	38f	"Lady"	Tenn.
, Lucy	16f		Ala.
, Molly	9f		Ala.
, James L.	6m		Tenn.
Story, N. M.	24m	overseer /970	Ga.
Kirkland, Annie	40f	com Gramer School	Boston Mass
Goree, Emma	6f		Tenn.

> Households 648 and 640 contain the family of R. H. Douglas 65m, retired, born Va. and his two propertied sons A. O. and Thomas E., both 31 years old, born Ark., cotton planters.

> Household 663 contained wealthy cotton planter Thomas Smith and his son Samuel G. who had moved to Auburn from Nashville, Tennessee.

17. Heavily armed, as armed "head to foot."

in it. In time, of course, I became used to it; and, considering their anxieties, the malarial climate, and the irritating "ague-cake,"[18] they behaved well, on the whole. Their general attitude was, however, stiff and constrained. Each slightly raised his hat as he came in, and their "Sirs" were more formal and punctilious than, as neighbours or fellow-citizens, they ought to have been.

My proud fellow-clerks were disposed to think it was the dread of the pistol which made them so guarded in speech and action, but I thought that it was the fear of compromising the personal dignity by a disgraceful squabble with men untaught in the forms of good society. Arkansas is sometimes known as the Bear State, and many of its people at that time were singularly bearish and rude. The self-estimate of such men was sometimes colossal, and their vanities as sensitive as hair-triggers. None of them could boast of the piety of saints, but nearly all had been influenced by the religion of their mothers—just as much as might enable them to be distinguished from barbarians. It is wonderful what trivial causes were sufficient to irritate them. A little preoccupation in one's own personal affairs, a monosyllabic word, a look of doubt, or a hesitating answer, made them flare up hotly. The true reason for this excessive sensitiveness was that they had lived too much within their own fences, and the taciturnity engendered by exclusiveness had affected their habits. However amiable they might originally have been, their isolation had promoted the growth of egotism and self-importance. This is the essence of "Provincialism," wherever it is met with, in country or in city life.

Few visited our store who did not bear some sign of the pernicious disease which afflicted old and young in the bottom lands of the Arkansas. I had not been a week at the store before I was delirious from the fever which accompanies ague,[19] and, for the first time in my life, was dieted on calomel and quinine. The young physician of our neighbour-

18. "Probably more or less enlargement of the spleen occurs in all cases of malarial fever. The enlargement is often sufficient for the organ to be readily felt through the abdominal walls, constituting what is commonly known as the 'Ague-cake' " (Austin Flint, *A Treatise on the Principles and Practice of Medicine*, 7th ed. [Philadelphia: Lea Brothers, 1894], 953).

19. "Ague" was a generic term at the time, usually referring to some form of malarial fever. "Anaemia is incident to the disease. . . . The patient complains of indefinite ailments, to which the term *bilious* is frequently applied" (ibid., 953–54).

hood, who boarded with Mr. Altschul,[20] communicated to me many particulars regarding the nature of this plague. In the form termed by him "congestive chills," he had known many cases to terminate fatally within a few hours. Blacks as well as white were subject to it. Nothing availed to prevent an attack. The most abstemious, temperate, prudent habits no more prevented it than selfish indulgence or intemperance. So, what with isolation on their wide estates, their life amongst obsequious slaves, indigestion, and inflamed livers, their surroundings were not well adapted to make our wealthy customers very amiable or sociable.

Though I had a bowing acquaintance with scores, only half-a-dozen or so people condescended to hold speech with me. The mention of these reminds me that one day one of my friends, named Newton Story,[21] and myself were weighed in the scales, and while Story, a fine manly fellow, weighed one hundred and eighty-five pounds, I was only ninety-five pounds,—within three pounds of seven stone. The frequency of ague attacks had reduced me to skin and bone. It was a strange disease, preceded by a violent shaking, and a congealed feeling as though the blood was suddenly iced, during which I had to be half-smothered in blankets, and surrounded by hot-water bottles. After a couple of hours' shivering, a hot fit followed, accompanied by delirium, which, about the twelfth hour, was relieved by exhausting perspiration. When, about six hours later, I became cool and sane, my appetite was almost ravenous from quinine and emptiness. For three or four days afterwards, unless the fever was tertian,[22] I went about my duties as before, when, suddenly, a fit of nausea would seize me, and again the violent malady overpowered me. Such was my experience of the agues of the Arkansas swamp-land; and, during the few months I remained at Cypress Bend, I suffered from them three times a month.[23]

20. The 1860 Census of Arkansas County, Arkansas, HH 599 (Altschur), Douglas township, South Bend post office, lists: "S. W. Jones, 23, male, Physician, $450 (personal property), born Georgia."

21. Newton M. Story was born about 1836 in Georgia, and in 1860 was the overseer on the farm of James L. Goree (1860 Census of Arkansas County, Arkansas, HH 639).

22. With a tertian fever "the interval is about forty-eight hours, or the paroxysm recurs on the third day" (Flint, *Principles and Practice of Medicine*, 952).

23. Later, when HMS had become a celebrity, many would claim a relationship with him as a young man. One of these curious stories attempts to deny his well-documented stay at Cypress Bend, indeed his service with the Sixth Arkansas Infantry. Nevertheless the tale gained some currency in Arkansas when HMS began making his American tours

The population of the State in that year (1861) was about 440,000; and I find, to my astonishment, that now (1895) it is over a million and a quarter, of whom only about 10,000 are foreign-born.[24] Neither the dreadful ague, which exceeds in virulence the African type, nor the Civil War, has been able to check the population. What a hope for much-scorned Africa there is in these figures!

But this is a digression due to my desire to be just to my bilious fellow-sufferers in the swamp-land. One of our new salesmen was famous as a violinist, and his favourite song and tune was about the "Arkansas Traveller," who, losing his way in one of the sloughy highways through the swamp, disappeared in the mud leaving his hat behind him to indicate the spot. Reflective people will see in this story another obstacle to social intercourse.

Every new immigrant soon became infected with the proud and sensitive spirit prevailing in Arkansas. The poor American settler, the Irish employee, the German-Jew storekeeper, in a brief time grew as liable to bursts of deadly passion, or fits of cold-blooded malignity, as the Virginian aristocrat. In New Orleans, and other great cities, the social rule was to give and take, to assert an opinion, and hear it contradicted without resort to lethal weapons, but, in Arkansas, to refute a statement was tantamount to giving the lie direct, and was likely to be followed by an instant appeal to the revolver or bowie. Sometimes an "*if* you said so, then I said so," staved off the bloody arbitrament, but such folk were probably late immigrants and not old citizens.

---

as a lecturer. Photographs of HMS were recognized, and a former Confederate officer, Capt. Marshall Stoddard, claimed to have known him as 1st Lt. J. C. Stanley, Fort Smith Rifles (Second Arkansas Trans-Mississippi Cavalry). Another Confederate agreed with Stoddard as did some of this Stanley's former pupils. At least they thought the photographs looked like the Stanley they had known. It seemed that this Stanley had participated, as a newspaper correspondent, in the expedition against the Mormons in 1857. He then came to Fort Smith in 1859 and taught at the J. M. War School until the outbreak of the war. He disgraced himself as a Confederate by displaying cowardice at the Battle of Oak Hill. Afterward he became an officer in Company A (C. Arthur Carroll's cavalry regiment). When entrusted with the company payroll during the winter of 1862 to 1863, he took a large portion of the money and fled to Mexico, and was not seen again until he supposedly resurfaced as the famous explorer (W. J. and J. F. Weaver, "Early Days in Fort Smith," typescript in Fort Smith Public Library, Fort Smith, Arkansas).

24. Officially Arkansas is shown in 1860 as having a population of 435,000; in 1880, 803,000; and in 1890, 1,128,000, (United States Department of Commerce, *Historical Statistics of the United States*. [Washington, D.C.: Government Printing Office, 1975], 2:24).

It struck even a youth like me as being ridiculous for a servile German-Jew peddlar to fancy himself insulted by a casual remark from some mean and ill-bred white, and to feel it necessary to face the tube of a backwoodsman, when he might have ignored him and his rudeness altogether. It was hard to understand why he should resent his honour being doubted, except from a mistaken sense of his importance, for the ill-opinion of the planter community he had trebly earned already, by being a trader, a foreigner, and a Jew; and the small portion of regard he aspired to win by an act of daring bluff was not worth a thought, least of all the peril of his life, or the smart of a wound. With regard to his "honour," it seemed to bear a different meaning on different banks of a river. On the eastern shore of the Mississippi, it meant probity in business; on the western shore, it signified popular esteem for the punishment of a traducer, and he who was most prompt in killing anyone who made a personal reflection obtained most honour, and therefore every peddlar or clerk in Arkansas hastened to prove his mettle.

At South Bend, about nine miles below us, there was a store-keeper who prided himself more upon the "honour" he had won as a duellist than upon commercial integrity. It was the example of his neighbourhood which had fired this abnormal ambition, and, on my arrival at the Arkansas, his clerks had begun to imitate him. The neighbouring merchants, envious of his fame, essayed the perilous venture; and, at last, Mr. Altschul was smitten with the mania. There is no doubt that, had his courage been of a more compact quality, he would have competed with the man of South Bend for "honour." He selected, however, the choicest of his stock of Smith and Wesson's vest-pocket revolvers, and was lavishly extravagant with the ammunition. At the outset, he could not resist blinking at the flash of his own pea-shooter, but, by dint of practice, he succeeded in plugging a big tree at twenty paces. Then, in an evil moment, his mounting spirit was inspired to turn his pistolette on a motherly old sow which had strayed among his cabbages, and he mortally wounded her. The owner of the animal was cross old Mr. Hubbard,[25] a small planter, who came on an ambling mule, presently, with a double-barrel shot-gun, charged with an awful number of buck-

---

25. Forty-two-year-old Eli J. Hubbard turns out to be one of the wealthiest planters in the area—$210,000 in real property, $100,000 in personal, a Tennessean with a wife and seven children, but listed oddly as "Overseer" (1860 Census of Arkansas County, Arkansas, HH 600).

pellets, to interview Mr. Altschul. When he returned home, I inferred, from Hubbard's satisfied smile, that the interview had not been unsatisfactory to him. From that moment we noticed that Mr. Altschul abandoned pistol practice—for, naturally, the pistolette was not a fit weapon to cope with a shot-gun. One of my fellow-clerks remarked that it was a pity Mr. Hubbard had no excuse for calling upon the man at South Bend for damages.

If the craze for shooting had been communicated to such a respectable man as Mr. Altschul, it may be imagined what a fascination pistols had for us youths. We had hip-pockets made in our trousers, and the Smith and Wesson was regarded as an indispensable adjunct to manhood. Our leisure hours were devoted to target-practice, until my proficiency was so great that I could sever a pack-thread at twenty paces. Theoretically, we were already man-slaughterers, for our only object in practice was to be expert in killing some imaginary rowdy, or burglar. In our rude world such a person might present himself at any moment. The rowdy needed only a little liquor to develop himself, and the store, guarded only by a boy at night, offered a tempting inducement to a burglarious individual. Among our hundred and odd customers there were several who were not over-regardful of our susceptibilities; and as my colleagues were of their own kidney, and had an acute sense of their dignity, there was no saying when a crisis might arise. Personally, I was not yet wrought up to this fine susceptiveness, though, probably, I had as quick a spirit as any fire-eater in Arkansas County. What I might do if my patience was abused, or how much bullying would be required to urge me to adopt the style in vogue, was, however, as yet undetermined. Of the code of honour and usage I had heard enough, but whenever I supposed myself to be the object of rude aggression, the dire extreme made me shrink. The contingency was a daily topic, but, when I dwelt on the possibility of being involved, I inwardly held that liquory ebullience ought not to be noticed.

Among our customers was a man named Coleman, a large, loose-jointed young fellow, who owned a plantation and some twenty slaves. At regular intervals he came to make his purchase of cloth for his slaves, provisions, etc., and always departed with a bottle of whiskey in each saddle-bag. One day he and some chance acquaintance had commenced a bottle of Bourbon, and under the influence of the liquor he became objectionable, and hinted to one of the salesmen that it was "rot-gut," diluted with swamp-water. At the commencement it was taken to be the rough pleasantry of a drunken rustic; but, as Coleman reiterated the charge, the clerk's patience was exhausted, and he retorted that swamp-water was wholesome for drunkards such as he. After this, one savage retort provoked another, and Coleman drew his revolver; but, as he aimed it, I crooked his elbow, and the bullet pierced the roof. Almost immediately after, the clerk had flung himself against his opponent, and we all three came to the floor. Then, while I clung to his thumb, to prevent his raising the hammer, assistance came from the next store-room; and the one who most efficiently interfered was a strong and stalwart planter, named Francis Rush, for he wrenched the weapon from his hand. There followed a disagreeable quarter of an hour: both Coleman and the clerk were wild to get at each other, but in the end we forced a truce. Coleman's saddle-bags were put on his horse, and I held his stirrups while he mounted. He glared fiercely at me awhile, and then, after a warning that I had better avoid meddling with other people's quarrels, he rode away.

Coleman never returned to the store again. Some weeks after this event, I was despatched round the neighbourhood to collect debts, and his name was on my list. There was an ominous silence about his house as I rode up, but, on making my way to the negro quarter to make enquiries, I was told in a frightened whisper that their master had disappeared into parts unknown, after killing Francis Rush.[26]

An evening came when the long-expected burglarious adventure occurred. Night had fallen by the time I returned to the store from supper at Mr. Altschul's, but there was a moonlight which made the dead timber in the Cypress Grove appear spectral. Near the main entrance to the store was a candle, which I proceeded to light after entering the building. Then, closing and dropping the strong bar across the door, I walked down the length of the store towards the office and my bedroom. Holding the candle well up, I noticed as I passed the fire-place a pile of soot

26. HMS seems to have the incident confused, certainly as to the names of the participants. No Coleman nor Francis Rush nor Coleman Rush appear in the vicinity, according to the 1860 Census, only a farmer named William S. Rush, age forty-four, born in South Carolina. The following unusual entry, however, does appear: "Martha Owenby, 43, female, farmer, $5,300/$13,505, born in South Carolina with 4 children, a carpenter and an overseer." Also listed in same household: "Frances Owenby 42, farmer killed by Colman Rush with double-barreled shotgun on August 2nd" (1860 Census of Arkansas County, Arkansas, HH 644).

on the hearth-stone. As it had been swept clean after the day's business, the sight of it instantly suggested a burglar being in the chimney. Without halting, I passed on to the office, cast a quick look at the back door and windows, and, snatching my little revolver from under the pillow, retraced my steps to the fire-place. Pointing the weapon up the chimney, I cried out, "Look out, I am about to fire. After the word 'three' I shall shoot. One! two!"—A cloud of soot poured down on my arm, the rumble of a hasty scramble was heard, and I fired into the brick to hasten his departure. I then flew into the office, set my candle upon a chair, opened the back-door, and darted out in time to see a negro's head and shoulders above the chimney-top. By means of threats, and a sufficient demonstration with the fire-arm, he was made to descend, and marched to Mr. Altschul's house, where he surrendered to the proprietor. Except that he was severely bound, his treatment was respectful, for he represented over a thousand dollars, and to injure him was to injure Dr. Goree, his owner, and one of our most respected customers.[27]

Mr. Altschul was an Israelite and kept open store on Sunday, for the benefit of the negroes around. The clerks, being Christians, were, of course, exempted from labour that day; but, on one special Sunday, one of our party had volunteered to take Mr. Altschul's place at the counter. In the afternoon, he was attending a clamouring crowd of about thirty negroes, with his counter littered with goods. As I came in, I observed that he was not so alertly watchful as he ought to have been, with such a number of men, and so many exposed articles. I sat down and closely watched, and saw that, each time his back was turned, two men abstracted stockings, thread-spools, and ribands, stuffing them into their capacious pockets. After considering the best method of compelling restoration, I withdrew and called Simon, Mr. Altschul's burly slave, and instructed him how to assist me.

A few seconds after re-entering the store, the two halves of the front door were suddenly flung to, and barred, and a cry of "Thieves" was raised. There was a violent movement towards me, but Simon flourished a big knife above his head, and swore he would use it, if they did not stand still and be searched. Those who were conscious of their in-

27. James Langston Goree had "organized Marion Institute, in Marion, Alabama, and became its first president and teacher of mathematics." He also had studied medicine before moving to Auburn (Victoria Cross, "The Goree Family," *Arkansas Historical Quarterly* 12 [summer 1953]: 117).

nocence sided with us; and through their help we turned out a pretty assortment of small goods, which the clerk, by referring to his sales-book, found had not been sold.

I went out to shoot turtle-doves one holiday, and aimed at one on a branch about thirty feet above the road, and over-hanging it. Almost immediately after, old Hubbard, the planter, emerged into view from round the corner, in a tearing rage, and presented his shot-gun at me. Seeing no one else near, and assuming that he was under some great mistake, I asked what the matter was, upon which he boldly accused me of shooting at him, and he put his hand to his face to show the wound. As there was not the slightest trace of even a bruise, I laughed at him, as it seemed to me that only an overdose of whiskey could account for such a paroxysm of passion.

Since my arrival at Auburn I had received three letters from my father from Havana, within a period of about nine weeks. Then, month after month of absolute silence followed. The last letter had stated that his brother was convalescent, and that, in about a month, he intended to return to New Orleans, and would then pay me a visit. Until well into March, 1861, I was in daily expectation of hearing from him, or seeing him in person. But we were destined never to meet again. He died suddenly in 1861—I only heard of his death long after.[28] In the mean time, wholly unheeded by me, astounding national events had occurred. Several of the Southern States had openly defied the United States Government. Forts, arsenals, and ships of war had been seized by the revolted States, and, what was of more importance to me, the forts below New Orleans had been taken by the Louisiana troops. These events were known to readers of newspapers in Arkansas, but the only newspaper taken at the Auburn store was a Pine Bluff weekly, which, as I seldom saw it, I never imagined would contain any news of personal interest to me.

28. According to McLynn, this is how HMS "simply 'killed off' his protector . . . and ended his connection with the Stanley family from whom he had taken his name." HHS did not die until November 1, 1878 (six months following his wife's death), age "sixty-seven, at Foley Plantation, in Assumption parish on Bayou Lafourche. He left an estate of $130,000 but not a penny of it went to his adopted son. Henry Hope gave instructions after the quarrel in 1859–60 that Stanley's name was never again to be mentioned in his presence" (McLynn, *Stanley*, 37. See also Bierman, *Dark Safari*, 27; *New Orleans Daily Picayune*, November 3, 10, 1878; Dillon, "From Wharf Waif to Knighthood," *Roosevelt Review*, 29–30).

It was not until March that I began dimly to comprehend that something was transpiring which would involve every individual. Dr. Goree,
our neighbour planter, happened to meet Mr. W. H. Crawford, an ex-
Representative of Georgia,[29] at our store, and began discussing politics.
Their determined accents and resolute gestures roused my curiosity,
and I heard them say that the States of Alabama, Georgia, Louisiana,
and others, had already formed a separate government, and that one
called Jeff Davis had been proclaimed President of the new government; and they wondered why Arkansas was so slow to join the Confederates, etc., etc. This was news to me, and when they unfolded their
respective newspapers and read extracts from them, it dawned upon me
that if I wished to post myself upon the grave national affairs, I should
have to read those stupid sheets which hitherto I had regarded as being
only fit for merchants and bearded men.

Thus stimulated to think that the events of the time affected the people of Arkansas County, even youths like myself, I began to read the
Pine Bluff paper, and to be more inquisitive; and it was not long before
I had a vague conception that the country was in a terribly disturbed
state, and that there would be war. Notwithstanding the information
gleaned from persons who gave themselves little trouble to satisfy a
strange boy, it was not until young Dan Goree returned from Nashville
College that I could assimilate properly all that I had heard.[30] Young
Dan was a boy of about my own age, and being the son of such a politi-
cian as Dr. Goree, was naturally much more advanced in political matters than I. He it was who, in friendly converse, acted as my Mentor,
and gave me the first intelligent exposition of how affairs stood between
the two sections of the Union. It was from him I learned that the election of Abe Lincoln, in the November previous, had created a hostile
feeling in the South, because this man had declared himself opposed to
slavery; and as soon as he became President, in March, he would do all
in his power to free all the slaves. Of course, said he, in that event all

29. The Georgian William H. Crawford did live on a farm near Auburn with his wife,
Caroline, and five children, but the well-known congressman William Harris Crawford
he purported to be had died almost thirty years earlier.

30. Although he also is listed as Dan D. Goree in Confederate service records, it appears he was named Don Dixon Goree, eldest son of James L. Dixon and Mary Elizabeth
Dixon. He was drowned, probably during the Civil War (Cross, "The Goree Family,"
117).

slave-holders would be ruined. His father owned about one hundred and twenty slaves, worth from $500 to $1200 a head, and to deprive him of property that he had bought with cash was pure robbery. That was the reason that all the people of the South were rising against the Northern people, and they would fight, to the last man. When the State of Arkansas "seceded," then every man and boy would have to proceed to the war and drive those wretched Abolitionists back to their homes, which would be an easy task, as one Southerner was better than ten of those Northern fellows, many of whom had never seen a gun! Dan thought that the boys of the South, armed with whips, would be quite sufficient to lick the thieving hounds!

I need not pursue the theme, but it was from such a source that I obtained my elementary lessons in American Politics. From the time when, in December, 1857, I had read some leaderette about the Louisiana Legislative Assembly, politics had been repulsively dry to me, and newspapers were only useful for their shipping and trade details.

Specially interesting to me, however, was it to know that Missouri and its metropolis, St. Louis, would assuredly join the South; though I was saddened to learn that Cincinnati and Louisville were enemies. What curious emotions that word "enemies" caused in me! People I knew well, with whom I had worshipped, boys with whom I had contracted delightful friendships at Newport and Covington,[31] to be enemies! Then I wondered how we were to obtain our goods in future. Consignments of arms, medicine, dry-goods, and ironware, had come to us from St. Louis, Cincinnati, and even Chicago. The conditions of trade would be altogether altered!

It was not, however, until I had propounded the question as to how the seizure of the Mississippi forts affected people who were abroad, and wished to return home, that I understood how deeply involved I was by this rupture of relations between the North and South. I was told that all communication was stopped, that ships coming in from sea would be turned back, or else, if they were permitted to come in by the cruisers outside, would certainly not be permitted to leave; that every ship insisting on going to New Orleans would be searched, and, if anything likely to assist the enemy was found, she would be detained, and

31. HMS refers to the river towns on the south bank of the Ohio opposite Cincinnati.

perhaps confiscated; and that, as no vessel was permitted to enter the river, so none would have the privilege of leaving. Here was something wholly unexpected! My father was shut out, and I was shut in! He could not come to me, nor could I join him. In some mysterious way somebody had built an impassable wall round about us, and the South was like a jail, and its inhabitants had been deprived of the liberty of leaving. From the moment that I fully realised this fact, everything bore a different aspect to what it had before. I was a strange boy in a strange land, in the same condition of friendlessness as when I fled from the *Windermere*. I had prepared myself to convince my father that the valley of the Arkansas was not a fit place to live in. My staring bones and hollow eyes should speak for me, and we would try the Washita Valley, or ascend the Arkansas, towards Little Rock, where the country was healthier, but anywhere rather than in such a pestilential place as the swamp-land of Arkansas. But my intentions had come to naught, my cherished hopes must be abandoned. I was stranded effectually, and I had no option but to remain with Mr. Altschul.

It was an evil hour to meditate any design of a personal nature, for the sentiment of the period was averse from it. The same unperceivable power that had imprisoned me in the fever-and-ague region of Arkansas was rapidly becoming formidable. Man after man unresistingly succumbed to its influence. Even the women and children cried for war. There was no Fiery Cross, but the wire flashed the news into every country-place and town, and, wherever two met, the talk was all about war. Most of the cotton States had already seceded, and as our State was their sister in sentiment, habit, and blood, Arkansas was bound to join her sisters, and hasten with her sons to the battle-field, to conquer or die. Early in May, the State Representatives met at Little Rock, and adopted the ordinance of secession;[32] whereupon the fighting spirit of the people rose in frenzy. Heroic sayings, uttered by ancient Greek and Roman heroes, were mouthed by every stripling. The rich planters forgot their pride and exclusiveness, and went out and orated among the common folk. They flourished their hats and canes, and cried, "Give us Liberty, or give us Death!" The young men joined hands and shouted,

32. The Ordinance of Secession was passed by the Arkansas State Convention May 6, 1861 (Clement A. Evans, ed., *Confederate Military History* [Atlanta: Confederate Publishing, 1899], 10:15).

"Is there a man with soul so dead, Who never to himself hath said— This is my own, my native land?" "An honourable death is better than a base life," etc., etc.[33] In the strident tones of passion, they said they would welcome a bloody grave rather than survive to see the proud foe violating their altars and their hearths, and desecrating the sacred soil of the South with their unholy feet. But, inflamed as the men and youths were, the warlike fire that burned within their breasts was as nothing to the intense heat that glowed within the bosoms of the women. No suggestion of compromise was possible in their presence. If every man did not hasten to the battle, they vowed they would themselves rush out and meet the Yankee vandals. In a land where women are worshipped by the men, such language made them war-mad.

Then one day I heard that enlistment was going on. Men were actually enrolling themselves as soldiers! A Captain Smith, owner of a plantation a few miles above Auburn, was raising a Company to be called the "Dixie Greys." A Mr. Penny Mason, living on a plantation below us, was to be the First-lieutenant, and Mr. Lee,[34] nephew of the great General Lee was to be Second-lieutenant. The youth of the neighborhood were flocking to them and registering their names. Our Doctor— Weston Jones,[35] Mr. Newton Story,[36] and the brothers Varner,[37] had enlisted. Then the boy Dan Goree prevailed upon his father to permit

33. HMS is quoting from Sir Walter Scott's *The Lay of the Last Minstrel*, canto 4, stanza 1.

34. Robert D. Lee, nineteen, enlisted with HMS and quickly became a sergeant. He was elected first lieutenant May 10, 1862, following Shiloh. That winter he would be sent back to Arkansas to recruit, only to be captured December 28, 1863, in Arkansas County and imprisoned at Johnson's Island (R. D. Lee Compiled Service Record [CSR]).

35. Starling Weston Jones, twenty-three, appears in the 1860 census in the household of Isaac Altshur with HMS. This young Georgian apparently enlisted as a private with the Dixie Grays, then became an assistant surgeon, and eventually surgeon. Reported killed at Resaca, he lived to be paroled at Greensboro in April 1865 (1860 Census of Arkansas County, Arkansas, Douglas township, South Bend post office, HH 599; CSR of Confederate General and Staff Officers and Nonregimental Enlisted Men, M331, Roll 144, NA).

36. Newton M. Story, twenty-four, born in Georgia, was overseer on the plantation of James L. Goree at Auburn. Story enlisted with HMS in Company E and quickly rose to sergeant. It is odd that HMS does not mention Story being killed at Shiloh on April 6, 1862 (1860 Census of Arkansas County, Arkansas, Auburn post office, HH 639; N. M. Story CSR).

37. Only one Varner brother was found in the rolls of the Sixth Arkansas: Pvt. A. H. Varner, Company E. He enlisted October 28, 1861, at Cave City, Kentucky, but became ill and was hospitalized in Atlanta. He is shown in the 1860 Arkansas County census as

him to join the gallant braves. Little Rich, of Richmond Store, gave in his name.[38] Henry Parker, the boy nephew of one of the richest planters in the vicinity, volunteered, until it seemed as if Arkansas County was to be emptied of all the youth and men I had known.

About this time, I received a parcel which I half-suspected, as the address was written in a feminine hand, to be a token of some lady's regard; but, on opening it, I discovered it to be a chemise and petticoat, such as a negro lady's-maid might wear. I hastily hid it from view, and retired to the back room, that my burning cheeks might not betray me to some onlooker. In the afternoon, Dr. Goree called, and was excessively cordial and kind. He asked me if I did not intend to join the valiant children of Arkansas to fight? and I answered "Yes."[39]

At my present age, the whole thing appears to be a very laughable affair altogether; but, at that time, it was far from being a laughing matter. He praised my courage, and my *patriotism*, and said I should win undying glory, and then he added, in a lower voice, "We shall see what we can do for you when you come back."

What *did* he mean? Did he suspect my secret love for that sweet child who sometimes came shopping with her mother? From that confidential promise I believed he did, and was, accordingly, ready to go anywhere for her sake.[40]

---

age twenty-six, "Dr. of Medasin," and overseer, residing in the home of his elder brother W. T. Varner. Both brothers were born in Georgia (A. H. Varner CSR; 1860 Census of Arkansas County, Arkansas, HH 608).

38. Rudolph Rich, seventeen, enlisted with HMS. He would be killed at Murfreesboro December 31, 1862 (R. Rich CSR).

39. Biographers of HMS disagree on the credibility of the Arkansas episode. McLynn believes it "obscure both in provenance and in chronology" and "a tangled deliberately obfuscated skein, of which only the main outlines are visible." Bierman, on the other hand, contends that the "sharp perceptions of Stanley's Cypress Bend reminiscences are in refreshing contrast to the sanctimonious implausibilities of his recollections of New Orleans," noting HMS's piercing observations of plantation owners and his caustic attitude toward the code of the southern gentleman. Hall echoes Bierman's sentiments: HMS "gives a telling portrait of life in the South on the eve of the Civil War" (McLynn, *Stanley*, 38–39; Bierman, *Dark Safari*, 30–32; Hall, *Stanley*, 124).

40. Hall and Bierman believe the chemise and petticoat to have been sent by Margaret Goree, a cousin of Dan's. Bierman writes, "She had seemed more friendly and sympathetic, and quieter, than the other local girls." They contend HMS was "secretly enamored" of her. Shuey, cited by Bierman for this information, provides no sources in her article about young Stanley, relying almost entirely upon the *Autobiography*. The young girl may have been Lucy Goree, age sixteen, or Molly, age nine, who would become the wife of Newton Story (Bierman, *Dark Safari*, 32; Hall, *Stanley*, 124; Mary Willis

About the beginning of July we embarked on the steamer "Frederick Notrebe." At various landings, as we ascended the river, the volunteers crowded aboard; and the jubilation of so many youths was intoxicating. Near Pine Bluff, while we were making merry, singing, "I wish I was in Dixie," the steamer struck a snag which pierced her hull, and we sank down until the water was up to the furnace-doors. We remained fixed for several hours, but, fortunately, the "Rose Douglas" came up, and took us and our baggage safely up to Little Rock.

We were marched to the Arsenal, and, in a short time, the Dixie Greys were sworn by Adjutant-General Burgevine[41] into the service of the Confederate States of America for twelve months. We were served with heavy flint-lock muskets, knapsacks, and accoutrements, and were attached to the 6th Arkansas Regiment of Volunteers, Colonel Lyons commanding, and A. T. Hawthorn, Lieutenant-colonel.[42]

Shuey, "Young Stanley; Arkansas Episode," *Southwest Review* 27 [winter 1944]: 362; Cross, "The Goree Family," 117).

41. HMS writes, "General Burgevine was, in later years, Commander of the Mercenaries, in the Imperial Chinese army against the Taipings, and an ally of General (Chinese) Gordon, at one time. Dismissed by the Imperialists, he sought the service of the Taipings. Wearied of his new masters, he conceived a project of dethroning the Emperor, and reigning in his stead; he went so far as to try and tempt Gordon to be his accomplice!" HMS confuses Adjutant General Burgevin with his brother who was conspicuous in the Tai Ping Rebellion. Edmund Burgevin, who was adjutant general of Arkansas during the gubernatorial term of his brother-in-law Henry M. Rector (1860–1862), was a Little Rock merchant and a controversial political figure (Stanley, *Autobiography*, 166; John L. Ferguson to Nathaniel C. Hughes, Jr., December 14, 1998; Evans, *Confederate Military History*, 8).

42. Gov. Henry M. Rector had seized the Federal arsenal February 8, 1861, and its "spacious grounds became a convenient rendezvous and camping place for volunteers." The regiment was organized June 5, 1861, and on July 15 its members were transferred to the Confederate Army by the Military Board of Arkansas, taking the Confederate oath on July 26. They moved first to Pocahontas, Arkansas, where a deadly epidemic of measles broke out, then to Pitman's Ferry on the Current River, where they would come under the command of Gen. Thomas C. Hindman and the celebrated drillmaster Gen. William J. Hardee. After an abortive "invasion" of south-central Missouri, the regiment marched to New Madrid, Missouri, where they crossed by boat to Columbus on October 3. Soon after the Battle of Belmont, they moved to Cave City, Kentucky, where they spent the winter of 1861 to 1862. It was there that "their deep affection with Swett's Mississippi Battery was formed" (CSR of the Sixth Arkansas Volunteer Infantry; Evans, *Confederate Military History*, 11, 15, 56–57, 298–99; Marcus J. Wright, *Arkansas in the War, 1861–1865*, ed. A. C. McGinnis [Batesville, Ark.: Independence County Historical Society, 1963], 28, 51, 54–55).

5

Soldiering

I am now about to begin a period lasting about six years, which, were it possible, I should gladly like to re-live, not with a view of repeating its woes and errors, pains and inconsistencies, but of rectifying the mistakes I made. So far, I had made none of any importance; but enlisting in the Confederate service, because I received a packet of female clothes, was certainly a grave blunder. But who is able to withstand his fate or thwart the designs of Providence? It may have been time for me, getting close on to eighteen, to lose some of the soft illusions of boyhood, and to undergo the toughening process in the trail of war. Looking backward upon the various incidents of these six years, though they appear disjointed enough, I can dimly see a connection, and how one incident led to the other, until the curious and somewhat involved design of my life, and its purpose, was consummated. But this enlistment was, as I conceive it, the first of many blunders; and it precipitated me into a veritable furnace, from which my mind would have quickly recoiled, had I but known what the process of hardening was to be.

Just as the fine edge of boyish sensitiveness was blunted, somewhat, by the daring blasphemy of the *Windermere* officers, so modesty and tenderness were to be shocked, by intercourse with men who cast off sweet manners with their civilian clothes, and abandoned themselves to the rude style of military life. A host of influences were at work sapping moral scruples. The busy days, the painful events, the excitement of the camp, the general irreligiousness, the disregard of religious practice, the contempt for piety, the licentious humours of the soldiers, the reckless and lavish destruction of life, the gluttonous desire to kill, the devices and stratagems of war, the weekly preaching in defence of it, the example of my elders and superiors, the enthusiasm of beautiful women for strife—finally, all that was weak, vain, and unfixed in my own nature, all conspired to make me as indifferent as of my fellows to all sacred duties.

I had to learn that which was unlawful to a civilian was lawful to the soldier. The "Thou shalt not" of the Decalogue, was now translated "Thou shalt." Thou shalt kill, lie, steal, blaspheme, covet, and hate; for, by whatever fine names they were disguised, everyone practised these acts, from the President down to the private in the rear rank. The prohibition to do these things was removed, and indulgence in license and excess was permissible. My only consolation, during this curious "volte-face" in morality, was, that I was an instrument in the strong, forceful grip of circumstance, and could no more free myself than I could fly.

Heaven knows if any among the Dixie Greys can look at the acts of the war with my eyes. Not having been educated as I had been, nor become experienced afterwards in the ways of many lands, it is not likely any of them would. Many them went to the war as passionate patriots in the spirit of religious duty, blessed by their families; others with an appetite for glory, the desire of applause, a fondness for military excitement, or because they were infected with the general craze, or to avoid tedious toil, or from the wildness of youth, etc. It was passionate patriotism that was the rule, and brought to its standard all sorts and conditions of men; and it was this burning passion that governed all conduct, and moulded public life to its will.[1]

Now all men who knew our brigade commander [Brig. Gen. Thomas C. Hindman] will concede that, whatever virtues he may have had, ambition was his distinguishing characteristic. It was commonly said that he was a man of genius, could command a Department, or be a first-class Minister of War; but, from what I can recollect of him, he aimed at the highest office in the land, and was sufficiently unscrupu-

1. Great attention has been directed to the motivation of Civil War soldiers recently. For insight into this complex and highly subjective topic see the splendid, dispassionate studies of James M. McPherson, *For Cause and Comrades: Why Men Fought in the Civil War* (New York: Oxford University Press, 1997) and Gary W. Gallagher, *The Confederate War* (Cambridge, Mass.: Harvard University Press, 1997).

lous to establish himself as a dictator.[2] Colonel Lyons was purely and simply a soldier[3]; Lieutenant-Colonel A. T. Hawthorn was too vain of military distinction, and the trappings of official rank, to have stooped to be a patriot in the ranks;[4] but Captain S. G. Smith was a patriot of the purest dye, of the most patrician appearance, one of the finest and noblest types of men I have ever met: a man of stubborn honour and high principles, brave, and invariably gentle in demeanour and address.[5] Our First-lieutenant was a Mr. Penny Mason, a Virginian, bright, sol-

---

2. For a recent study of the controversial Hindman (1828–1868) see Diane Neal and Thomas W. Kremm, *The Lion of the South: General Thomas C. Hindman* (Macon, Ga.: Mercer University Press, 1993).

3. Richard Lyon was born about 1813 in Maryland. He is shown in the 1860 Census of Ouachita County, Arkansas, as a forty-seven-year-old lawyer, born in Maryland, living in Camden, Arkansas, with his wife, Mary (age forty-one), and two children. Captain of Company H, Sixth Arkansas Infantry, elected colonel June 5, 1861, he was killed the night of October 11, 1861, when his horse fell over a bluff into the Tennessee River near Bowling Green (Bruce S. Allardice to Nathaniel C. Hughes, Jr., November 20, 1998; Mamie Yeary, *Reminiscences of the Boys in Gray, 1861–1865* [Dallas: Smith & Lamar, 1912]).

4. Alexander Travis Hawthorn (1825–1899), a native of Alabama and a well-educated lawyer of Camden, Arkansas, would command the Sixth Arkansas following the death of Lyon, lead it at Shiloh, then move up to brigade command in June 1862. He would return to Arkansas in command of a brigade in Churchill's Division and remain there throughout the war. Following the war General Hawthorn emigrated to Brazil, returned and went into business in Atlanta, then about 1880 became a Baptist minister in Texas (Ezra J. Warner, *Generals in Gray: Lives of the Confederate Commanders* [Baton Rouge: Louisiana State University Press, 1959], 129–30. See also *Confederate Veteran* [*CV*] 5:68).

5. Samuel Granville Smith (ca. 1837–1864) was born in Tennessee, the son of Col. Thomas Smith and Elizabeth Robertson. After attending the University of Nashville, Smith settled near Auburn, Arkansas, with his father. They appear in the 1860 census as Thomas Smith, age sixty, cotton planter, $80,000 in real, $94,000 in personal property; and Samuel Smith, age twenty-three, "Gentleman," $2,000 in personal property. Samuel Smith raised the Dixie Grays and, following Shiloh, was elected major of the Sixth Arkansas and that May became colonel of the regiment. He was wounded at the Battle of Murfreesboro and captured at the Battle of Jonesboro September 1, 1864. Smith, a distant relative of Generals Cheatham and Hood, died September 28, 1864, in a Federal hospital of "remittant fever" and was buried near Atlanta (Bruce S. Allardice to Nathaniel C. Hughes, Jr., November 23, 1998; 1860 Census of Arkansas County, Arkansas, HH 633; S. G. Smith CSR; Weston Goodspeed, *Biographical and Historical Memoirs of Eastern Arkansas* [Chicago: Goodspeed Publishing Co., 1890], 637; United States War Department, *Supplement to the Official Records of the Union and Confederate Armies* [*OR Supp.*], ed. Janet B. Hewett, Noah A. Trudeau, and Bryce A. Suderow [Wilmington, N.C.: Broadfoot Publishing, 1994–], part 2, 2:386, 392; *CV*, 12:124).

dierly, zealous, and able, and connected with the oldest families of his State. He rose, as his military merits deserved, to the rank of Adjutant-general.[6] Our Second-lieutenant was a nephew of General Lee, who in the soldiers' parlance was a "good fellow." He also became distinguished during the war. Our Third-lieutenant was a "dandy," who took immense trouble with his appearance, and was always as neat as a military tailor and the laundry could make him.[7] Our Orderly-sergeant was an old soldier of the name of Armstrong, an honest and worthy fellow, who did his duty with more good-humour and good-nature than would have been expected under the circumstances.[8]

The privates were, many of them, young men of fortune, sons, or close relations, of rich Arkansas planters of independent means; others were of more moderate estate, overseers of plantations, small cotton-

6. Arthur Pendleton "Penny" Mason was born December 11, 1835, in Alexandria, Virginia. After attending the University of Virginia (1853–1855) he moved west and began planting and practicing law at Auburn, Arkansas. In 1860 he is shown residing alone near Auburn with real property valuing $60,000 and personal property $87,650. It appears Mason left the Sixth Arkansas at Columbus during the winter of 1861 to 1862, for on February 1, 1862, he is shown as a staff member to Gen. Joseph E. Johnston in Virginia. He was promoted to captain the following month and continued as assistant adjutant general (AAG) to Johnston until Lee took command of the Army of Northern Virginia. Mason served as one of Lee's staff from June 1862 until November 1862 when he returned to Johnston and was promoted to major. In early 1864 Mason is shown as a staff officer for Lt. Gen. Leonidas Polk in Mississippi, and by December 1864, he had been promoted to lieutenant colonel and was in Tennessee as AAG on John Bell Hood's staff. He ended the war as AAG to Joseph E. Johnston in North Carolina. Following the surrender Mason lived in New Orleans and died April 22, 1893 (Robert E. L. Krick to Nathaniel C. Hughes, Jr., November 23, 1998; A. P. Mason CSR; 1860 Census of Arkansas County, Arkansas, HH 645; Joseph H. Crute, Jr., *Confederate Staff Officers, 1861–1865* [Powhatan, Va.: Derwent Books, 1982], 104; United States War Department, *War of the Rebellion: A Compilation of the Official Records of the Union and Confederate Armies [OR]* [128 parts in 70 vols., Washington, D.C.: Government Printing Office, 1880–1901], 5:527; *CV*, 14:138; CSR of Confederate General and Staff Officers and Nonregimental Enlisted Men, M331, Roll 165, NA).

7. Charles F. Notrebe enlisted with HMS and was elected third lieutenant February 11, 1862. Prior to Shiloh he acted as adjutant to the regiment, but he would be dropped, probably at the time of consolidation (C. F. Notrebe CSR; *OR Supp.*, part 2, 2:386).

8. Orderly Sgt. James T. Armstrong was elected captain of Company E following Shiloh. He would be killed at the Battle of Murfreesboro December 31, 1862. He is shown in 1860 as a farmer, age thirty-four, born in Tennessee, with $12,000 in real and $22,000 in personal property, residing in Jefferson County, with his wife, Matilda, and four children (J. T. Armstrong CSR; 1860 Census of Jefferson County, Arkansas, HH 139).

growers, professional men, clerks, a few merchants, and a rustic lout or two. As compared with many others, the company was a choice one, the leaven of gentlehood was strong, and served to make it rather more select than the average.[9] Still, we were only a tenth of a regiment,[10] and, though a fifth of the regiment might be self-respecting, gentlemanly fellows, daily contact in camp with a majority of rough and untaught soldiers is apt to be perverting in time.

We were not subjected to the indignity of being stripped and examined like cattle, but were accepted into the military service upon our own assurance of being in fit condition; and, after being sworn in, we shed our civil costumes, and donned the light grey uniforms. Having been duly organized, we next formed ourselves into messes. My mess consisted of Jim Armstrong, the Orderly-sergeant; Newton Story, the Colour-sergeant, who had been overseer of Dr. Goree's plantation; Dan Goree, a boy, the son and heir of Dr. Goree;[11] Tom Malone, a genial fellow, but up to every gambling trick, a proficient in "High-low-jack," Euchre, Poker, and Old Sledge,[12] and, when angered, given to deliver himself in very energetic language;[13] old Slate, knowing as any, anecdotive [sic], and pleasant.[14] Tomasson, a boisterous fellow, who acted frequently like a bull in a china-shop, was admitted by Armstrong

9. Another company, Company A, the "Capitol Guards," produced many leaders in post-war Arkansas and is generally regarded as the premier company of the Sixth Arkansas Infantry.

10. Ten companies constituted an infantry regiment in 1861. Although some companies numbered as many as one hundred troops, the vast majority had only fifty to seventy-five effectives.

11. Pvt. Dan Dixon Goree, eighteen, was severely wounded at Shiloh and discharged on April 10, 1862 (D. D. Goree CSR. See also n. 30 in chapter 4).

12. Descended from the card game Triomphe or Trumps, Euchre (until 1857) was "little known except in the West and the South." It was the game for which the Joker was invented and was usually played with two competing partnerships. High-Low-Jack (All Fours) was played in England in the seventeenth century and taken up by the American colonials. Commonly known in the United States as Seven-up or Old Sledge, it was a favorite game and appears in the tales of Twain, Harte, and O. Henry. Eventually it would be supplanted by Poker (Albert H. Morehead, ed., *The Complete Hoyle*, rev. ed. [New York: Doubleday, 1991], 239, 311–12; David Parlett, *The Oxford Guide to Card Games* [New York: Oxford University Press, 1990], 190–91).

13. Pvt. W. T. Malone, twenty-one, enlisted with HMS, but became ill and was sent to Atlanta where he died March 9, 1862 (W. T. Malone CSR).

14. Pvt. James M. Slate enlisted with HMS and served in the Sixth Arkansas throughout the war (J. M. Slate CSR).

to the mess because he was a neighbour, and full of jests.[15] A Sibley tent, an improvement on the bell-tent, contained the whole of us comfortably.[16]

Dan Goree had brought his slave Mose, a faithful blackie to wait upon him. The mess annexed his services as cook and tin-washer, and, in return, treated Dan with high consideration. Mose was remarkable for a cow-like propensity to kick backward, if we but pointed our fingers at him. Armstrong contributed to the general comfort a stylish canteen and the favour of his company; and the rest of us gave our services and means to make the social circle as pleasant as possible, which, as we were "bright, smart, and alive," meant a great deal; for, if there were any fowls, butter, milk, honey, or other accessories to diet in our neighbourhood, they were sure to be obtained by some indefatigable member of the mess. I was too "green" in the forager's arts, at the beginning of the campaign, but I was apt; and, with such ancient campaigners as Armstrong and old Slate,—both of whom had been in the Mexican War of 1847,—I did not lack tuition by suggestion.

When clothed in our uniforms, each of us presented a somewhat attenuated appearance; we seemed to have lost in dignity, but gained in height. As I looked at Newton Story's form, I could scarcely believe my eyes. Instead of the noble portliness for which he had been distinguished, he was lean as a shorn sheep. Sleek Dan Goree was girlishly slender, while I had a waspish waist, which measured a trifle more than two hands. Dr. Jones was like a tall, over-grown lad; and, as for the Varner brothers, they were elegant to the verge of effeminacy.

With military clothes, we instinctively assumed the military pose: our heads rose stiff and erect above our shoulders, our chests bulged out, and our shoulder-blades were drawn in. We found ourselves cunningly peeping from the corners of our eyes, to observe if any admired our martial style. The Little Rock "gals," crowding about the Arsenal grounds,[17] were largely responsible for the impressive airs we took. The

15. Pvt. T. A. Thomasson, Company E, was killed at Shiloh on April 6. Pvt. C. H. Thomasson was in Company H (T. A. Thomasson CSR; C. H. Thomasson CSR).

16. Developed for the "old army" prior to the Civil War, this conical tent could accommodate twenty soldiers and their stove (see Patricia L. Faust, ed., *Historical Times Illustrated Encyclopedia of the Civil War* [New York: Harper & Row, 1986], 687–88).

17. For the purpose of drill and discipline the companies being raised in HMS's section of Arkansas went to Little Rock where they were quartered at the Arsenal and re-

prettiest among them drew into her circle a score or more of heroic admirers, whose looks pictured their admiration; and how envied were
they who obtained a smile from the fair! And how they strutted, with
their eyeballs humid with love! If, when we promenaded the streets,
with equal step and arm-in-arm, we detected the presence of cambric
frocks on a "stöep," or in some classic porch, we became as ridiculous
as peacocks from excess of vanity. Indeed, in those early days, we were
all over-troubled with patriotic thrills, sanguinary ardour, and bursts of
"bulliness." The fever of military enthusiasm was at its height, in man,
woman, and child; and we, who were to represent them in the war, received far more adulation than was good for us. The popular praise
turned our young heads giddy, and anyone who doubted that we were
the sanest, bravest, and most gallant boys in the world, would have been
in personal danger! Unlike the Spartans, there was no modesty in the
estimate of our own valour. After a few drills, we could not even go to
draw rations without the practice of the martial step, and crying out
"Guide centre," or "Right wheel," or some other order we had learned.
At our messes, we talked of tactics, and discussed Beauregard's and
Lee's merits, glorified Southern chivalry, and depreciated the Yankees,
became fluent in the jargon of patriotism, and vehement in our hatred
of the enemy. Few of us had ever smelled the fumes of battle, but that
did not deter us from vividly painting scenes of carnage when the blood
rolled in torrents, and the favoured "Dixie Greys" led the van to victory.[18]

Our martial souls were duly primed for the field by every adjunct of
military system. The fife, drum, and trumpet sounded many times a
day. A fine brass band thrilled us, morning and evening, with stirring
music. The drum and fife preceded us to the drilling-ground, and inspired us to sprightliness, campward. We burnished brass buttons,
arms, and accoutrements, until they shone like new gold. We bought

---

ceived into the service of the state. On hand were special mustering and medical officers.
It was here that Smith's Company E became one of the ten companies of the Sixth Arkansas Volunteer Infantry commanded by Col. Alexander T. Hawthorne (*OR*, 53:688, 702).

18. Officers of the Dixie Grays not mentioned by HMS are William F. Douglas, second lieutenant, who would be promoted to major in May 1862; J. M. Dulin, first lieutenant, who would become a staff officer under Hindman's successor St. John R. Liddell; Alf
F. Harrington, second lieutenant; and W. R. Gocio, second lieutenant (*OR Supp.*, part 2,
2:386, 392).

long Colt's revolvers, and long-bladed bowie-knives; we had our images taken on tin-types in our war-paint and most ferocious aspects, revolver in one hand, bowie-knife in the other, and a most portentous scowl between the eyebrows. We sharpened the points of our bayonets, and gave a razor-edge to our bowies, that the extermination we intended should be sudden and complete.

After a few weeks we made our last march through the Arkansan capital. The steamer was at the river-side, to take us across. The streets were gay with flags and ladies' dresses. The people shouted, and we, raw and unthinking, responded with cheers. We raised the song, "We'll live and die for Dixie," and the emotional girls waved their handkerchiefs and wept. What an imposing column we made! The regiment was in full strength. The facets of light on our shining muskets and bayonets were blinding. Banners of regiments and companies rustled and waved to the breeze. We strode down to the levee with "Eyes front," after the manner of Romans when reviewed by their tribunes!

Once across the river, that August day, we strapped our knapsacks, slung our haversacks and water-canteens, and felt more like veterans. All being ready, our physically-noble Colonel Hawthorn, prancing on his charger, drew his bright sword, and, after he had given us a sufficiently stern glance, rode to the head of the regiment; the brass band struck up a lively tune, and we swung gaily in column of four along the pike, towards the interior. Our officers and orderly walked parallel with us. The August sun was extremely hot, the pike was hard, dry, and dusty. At first, the officers' voices had a peremptory and sharp ring in them as they sang out, "Keep step, there! Left shoulder, shift arms! Dress up!" but after a while, as the heat began to force a copious perspiration, and the limy dust from the metalled highway parched our throats, they sobered down, and allowed us to march at ease.

Within an hour the sweat had darkly stained our grey coats about the arm-pits and shoulders, and it rolled in streams down our limbs into our boots, where, mingling with the dust and minute gravel, it formed a gritty mud which distressed our feet. Our shoulders ached with the growing weight and hardness of the muskets, our trousers galled us sorely, the straps and belts became painfully constrictive, and impeded respiration, but, through fear of shame, we endured all, without complaint. At the end of the hour we were halted for five minutes' rest, and then resumed the march.

Like all new recruits, we carried a number of things that veterans dispense with: for instance, keepsakes, and personal treasures; mine were a daguerreotype of my adopted father, and a lock of his grey hair,—very trivial and valueless to others, but my own peculiar treasures, carried in my knapsack to be looked at every Sunday morning when we smartened up. With these, toilet articles, soap, changes of under-clothing, camp-shoes, etc., besides extra uniform, and blankets, made up our luggage, which, with heavy musket, bayonet-accoutrements, and canteen of water, weighed about sixty pounds, and more, in some cases. For growing and lean youths this was a tremendous weight; and, during the second hour, the sense of oppression and soreness rapidly increased; but, excepting more frequent changes of the musket from shoulder to shoulder, we bated nothing of our resolve to endure.

After the second halt we were sensibly lamer. The gravel created blisters and the warm mud acted like a poultice on the feet. The military erectness gave way to a weary droop, and we leaned forward more. We were painfully scalded, restlessly shifted our weapons, and tried scores of little experiments, hustled our cartridge-pouches, inch by inch, then from back to front, from right to left; tugged at our breast-straps, eased our belts, drank copious draughts of water; and still the perspiration rolled in a shower down our half-blinded faces, and the symptoms of collapse became more and more pronounced.

Finally, the acutest point of endurance was reached, and nature revolted. Our feet were blistered, our agonies were unendurable, and, despite official warning and menace, we hopped to the road-side, whipped off our boots to relieve our burning feet; after a little rest, we rose and limped after the company. But the column had stretched out to a tremendous length with its long wagon-train, and to overtake our friends seemed hopeless. As we limped along, the still untired soldiers mocked and jeered at us, and this was very hard to endure. But, by and by, the stragglers became more numerous; the starch appeared to be taken out of the strongest, and, the longer the march continued, the greater was the multitude of the weary, who crawled painfully in the rear of the column.

Had the Little Rock ladies witnessed our arrival at camp late at night, we should have been shamed for ever. But, fortunately, they knew nothing of this; and blessing the night which hid our roasted faces and sorry appearance, we had no sooner reached the precincts of the camp than we embraced the ground, pains and aches darting through every tortured limb, feet blistered and bleeding, our backs scorched, and our shoulders inflamed. No bed that I had ever rested on gave me a tithe of the pleasure afforded me now by the cold, damp pasture-land.

The next day was a halt. Many of us were more fitted for hospital at day-break than for marching, but, after a bathe in the stream, a change of linen, and salving our wounds, we were in better mood. Then Armstrong, the old orderly, suggested that we should shed our knapsacks of all "rubbish," and assisted his friends by his advice as to what was indispensable and what was superfluous. The camp-fires consumed what we had rejected, and, when we noted the lightened weight of our knapsacks after this ruthless ransackment, we felt fitter for the march than on the day we departed from the Arkansas River.

Our surroundings at camp were novel for inexperienced youths. We were tented along the roadside, having taken down the fences of a field, and encroached on farmlands, without asking permission. The rails were also freely used by us as firewood. A town of canvas had risen as if by magic, with broad, short streets, between the company tents; and in the rear were located the wagons carrying provisions, ammunition, and extra equipments.

In a few days we were camped in the neighbourhood of Searcy, about sixty miles from Little Rock. The aspect of the country was lovely, but there was something fatal to young recruits in its atmosphere. Within two weeks an epidemic carried off about fifty, and quite as many more lay in hospital.[19] Whether it was the usual camp typhus, or malarious fever, aggravated by fatigue and wretched rations, I was too young to know or to concern myself about; but, in the third week, it seemed to threaten us all, and I remember how the soldiers resorted to the prayer-meetings in each company, and how solemn they were at service on Sunday. The pressure of an impending calamity lay heavy upon us all while in camp, but, as soon as we left it, we recovered our spirits.

19. Even after the Confederates established regular camps at Columbus (winter 1861 to 1862) and at Corinth (following Shiloh), disease continued to ravage the army. Although the number of deaths from disease at Columbus is unknown, the size of Confederate Cemetery supports the testimony of HMS. At Corinth, in mid-May 1862, "unsanitary conditions had already put at least twenty thousand men [of the Confederate Army of Tennessee] on the sick list" (Thomas L. Connelly, *Army of the Heartland: The Army of Tennessee, 1861–1862* [Baton Rouge: Louisiana State University Press, 1967], 176–77).

It was at this camp I acquired the art of diving. At swimming I was a proficient a long time before, but the acquisition of this last accomplishment soon enabled me to astonish my comrades by the distance I could traverse under water.

The brigade of General Hindman was at last complete in its organisation and consisted of four regiments, some cavalry, and a battery of artillery.[20] About the middle of September we moved across the State towards Hickman on the Mississippi, crossing the Little Red, White, Big Black, and St. Francis Rivers, by the way. Once across the Mississippi, we marched up the river, and, in the beginning of November, halted at what was then called "the Gibraltar of the Mississippi."[21]

On the 7th of November, we witnessed our first battle,—that of Belmont,—in which, however, we were not participants. We were held in readiness on the high bluffs of Columbus, from whence we had a commanding view of the elbow of land nearly opposite, whereon the battle took place. The metaphor "Gibraltar" might, with good reason, be applied to Columbus, for General Polk had made notable exertions to make it formidable. About one hundred and forty cannon, of large and small calibre, had been planted on the edge of the steep and tall bluffs opposite Belmont, to prevent the descent of the river by the enemy.

A fleet of vessels was discerned descending, a few miles above Belmont, and two gun-boats saucily bore down and engaged our batteries. The big guns, some of them 128-pound Parrott-rifled, replied with such a storm of shell that they were soon obliged to retreat again; but we novices were delighted to hear the sound of so many cannon. We received a few shots in return, but they were too harmless to do more than add to the charm of excitement. The battle began at between ten and eleven in the morning, the sky then being bright, and the day gloriously sunny; and it continued until near sunset. Except by the volleying thick haze which settled over the woods, we could not guess what was

20. By January 1862, Hindman's brigade consisted of the First, Second, and Sixth Arkansas Volunteer Infantries; the Third Confederate Infantry (the Nineteenth Arkansas Infantry combined with the First Arkansas Battalion under Col. John Marmaduke); and Charles Swett's four-gun Mississippi Battery. In addition Hindman oversaw the Second Kentucky Cavalry (commanded by Col. John H. Morgan) and the Eighth Texas Cavalry (commanded by Col. Benjamin F. Terry) (*OR*, 7:852).

21. Columbus with its towering bluffs was considered the most heavily fortified point in North America in the fall of 1861 (See Nathaniel C. Hughes, Jr., *The Battle of Belmont: Grant Strikes South* [Chapel Hill: University of North Carolina Press, 1991], 36–37).

occurring. The results were, on our side, under General Polk, 641 killed, wounded, and missing. On the Federal side, under General Grant, the loss was 610 killed, wounded, and missing.[22] To add to our casualties, a 128-pound rifled-gun burst at our battery by which seven of the gunners were killed, and General Polk and many of his officers were wounded.[23]

A youth requires to be educated in many ways before his manhood is developed. We have seen what a process the physical training is, by the brief description of the first day's march. It takes some time to bring the body to a suitable state for ungrudging acceptance of the hard conditions of campaigning, so that it can find comfort on a pike, or in a graveyard, with a stone for a pillow, and ease on clods, despite drenching rain and chilling dew. Then the stomach has to get accustomed to the soldier's diet of fried, or raw, bacon and horse-beans. The nerves have to be inured to bear, without shrinking, the repeated shocks and alarms of the camp. The spirit has to be taught how to subject itself to the spurns and contumely of superior and senior, without show of resentment; and the mind must endure the blunting and deadening of its sensibilities by the hot iron of experience.

During the long march from Little Rock to Columbus we became somewhat seasoned, and campaigning grew less and less unpleasant. Our ordinary march was now more in the nature of an agreeable relief from monotonous camp-duties. We were not so captious and ready to take offence as at first, and some things that were once most disagreeable were now regarded as diversions.

I now fully accepted it as a rule that a soldier must submit to military law; but many, like myself, had lost a great deal of that early enthusiasm for a soldier's life by the time we had reached Columbus.[24] It had struck us when at picket-duty alone, in the dark, that we had been great fools to place ourselves voluntarily in a position whence we could not retreat

22. Estimates of casualties at Belmont vary. Generally accepted figures are: Federal, 550 to 600; Confederate, 641 (ibid., 184–85).

23. For an account of the explosion of the "Lady Polk" on November 11, 1861, see ibid., 191.

24. For a complementary view of camp life at Columbus by another literate Arkansas private, during the fall and winter of 1861 to 1862, see Philip Daingerfield Stephenson, *The Civil War Memoir of Philip Daingerfield Stephenson*, ed. Nathaniel C. Hughes, Jr. (1995; reprint, Baton Rouge: Louisiana State University Press, 1998), 38–51.

without forfeit of life; and that, by a monosyllable, we had made our comrades our possible enemies upon a single breach of our oath. We had condemned ourselves to a servitude more slavish than that of the black plantation-hands, about whose condition North and South had declared war to the death. We could not be sold, but our liberties and lives were at the disposal of a Congress about which I, at least, knew nothing, except that, somewhere, it had assembled to make such laws as it pleased. Neither to Captain Smith, nor to Lieutenant Mason, nor even to my messmate Armstrong, could I speak with freedom. Any of them might strike me, and I should have to submit. They could make me march where they pleased, stand sentry throughout the night, do fatigue-duty until I dropped, load my back as they would a mule, ride me on a rail, make a target of me if I took a quiet nap at my post; and there was no possible way out of it.

To say the truth, I had not even a desire to shirk the duties I had undertaken. I was quite prepared and ready to do all that was required; for I loved the South because I loved my Southern friends, and had absorbed their spirit into every pore. Nevertheless, when far removed from the hubbub of camp, at my isolated post, my reason could not be prevented from taking a cynical view of my folly in devoting myself to be food for powder, when I might have been free as a bird, to the extent of my means. And if, among my vague fancies, I had thought that, by gallantry, I might win promotion such as would be some compensation for the sacrifice of my liberty, that idea had been exploded as soon as I had measured myself by hundreds of cleverer, abler, and braver men, and saw that they, even, had no chance of anything but to fill a nameless grave. The poetry of the military profession had departed under the stress of many pains, the wear and tear, and the certainty that soldiering was to consist of commonplace marches, and squalid camp-life.

The punishment inflicted on such as were remiss in their duties during the march had opened my eyes to the consequences of any misdemeanour, or an untimely ebullience of youthful spirits. I had seen unfortunate culprits horsed on triangular fence-rails, and jerked up by vicious bearers, to increase their pains; others, straddled ignominiously on poles; or fettered with ball and chain; or subjected to head-shaving; or tied up with the painful buck and gag; or hoisted up by the thumbs; while no one was free of fatigue-duty, or exempt from fagging to someone or other, the livelong day.

Those who were innocent of all breaches of "good order and discipline" had reason to lament having sacrificed their independence, for
our brigade-commander, and regimental officers, were eaten up with
military zeal, and were resolved upon training us to the perfection of
soldierly efficiency, and, like Bully Waters of the *Windermere*, seemed
to think that it was incumbent on them to get the full value of our keep
and pay out of us. They clung to the antiquated notion that soldiers
were appointed as much to drudge for their personal service as for the
purposes of war. Besides the morning and evening musters, the nine
o'clock dress-parade, the drill from that hour to noon, the cleaning of
arms and accoutrements, the frequent interruptions of rest by the "long
roll" heard in the dead of night, the guard-duty, or picket, we had to
cook our provisions, put up the officers' tents, make their beds soft as
straw and hay or grass could make them, collect fuel for their fires, dig
ditches around their tents, and fag for them in numberless ways. These
made a mighty list of harassments, which, on account of the miserably
hard fare, and insufficient preparation of it, weighed on our spirits like
lead, tended to diminish our number by disease, and sent hundreds to
the hospital.

The Dixie Greys, for instance, consisted mostly of young men and
lads who were as ignorant of the art of converting their ration of raw
beef and salt pork, field beans, and flour, into digestible food, as they
were of laundry work; yet they were daily served with rations, which
they might eat raw, or treat as they liked. Of course, they learnt how to
cook in time; but, meanwhile, they made sorry messes of it, and suffered
accordingly. Those with good constitutions survived their apprentice-
ship, and youth, open air, and exercise, enabled them to bear it a long
time; but when, with improper food, the elements chilled and heated us
with abrupt change, and arbitrary officialism employed its wits to keep
us perpetually on the move, it becomes evident, now, why only the har-
diest were enabled to bear the drudgery and vexation imposed upon
them, and why disease slew more than two-thirds of the whole number
of soldiers who perished during the war.

The fault of the American generalship was that it devoted itself
solely to strategy and fighting, and providing commissariat supplies; but
seldom, or never, to the kindly science of health-preservation. The officers knew how to keep their horses in good condition; but I do not
remember ever to have seen an officer who examined the state of our
messes, or stooped to show that, though he was our military superior,

he could take a friendly and neighbourly interest in our well-being, and that his rank had not estranged his sympathies. If, at the muster, a soldier was ill, he was put on the sick-list; but it never seems to have struck any officer, from General Lee down to the Third-lieutenant of an infantry company, that it might be possible to reduce the number of invalids by paying attention to the soldiers' joys and comforts. The raw provisions were excellent and abundant, and they only needed to be properly prepared to have made us robust and strong.

Just as the regimental physician and his assistants were requisite for the *cure* of illness, a regimental "chef," as superior of the company's cooks, would have been useful for the *prevention* of it, in fifty per cent of the cases; but the age was not advanced enough to recognise this.

Although I am apt to assign causes for things in my old age, it must not be supposed that I, as a boy, could then know much about such matters. I was, fortunately, blessed with the power of endurance, and was of so elastic a disposition that I could act my part without cavil or criticism. At that time, I felt that I had no other business in the world than to eat, work, and use my eyes, wits, and powers as a soldier, and to be as happy as my circumstances would allow; and I do not think I made myself obnoxious to any living soul. Within our mess we were not without our disagreements, and I had to bear my share of banter from my elders; but none can say, "This was he whom we had sometime in derision, and a proverb of reproach. We accounted his life madness, and his end to be without honour."[25]

The exigencies of war necessitated our removal by train from Columbus to Cave City, Kentucky, where we arrived about the 25th of November, 1861. We remained in this camp until about the middle of February, 1862. The force around Bowling Green and Cave City numbered 22,000. Our brigade was attached to the Division of General Hardee, author of "Tactics." During the time we remained there, no fighting occurred; but we made several midnight marches towards Green River, and posted ourselves in positions to surprise the enemy, expected to come from Munfordville.[26]

25. HMS appears to be paraphrasing verse 3, chapter 5, the Wisdom of Solomon from the Apocrypha.

26. On December 17, 1861, Hindman led a combined force (1,100 infantry, 250 cavalry, and Swett's four-gun battery) from his camp at Cave City towards Woodsonville, Kentucky. As the brigade approached Green River, fighting developed and the celebrated Col. Benjamin F. Terry (Eighth Texas Cavalry or more popularly Terry's Texas Rangers)

During the winter in this camp I won the approval of the mess by an aptitude for lessening the inconveniences under which we suffered in mid-winter, and my success in foraging. Instead of a fire under the Sibley tripod, which, besides endangering our feet and bedding, smoked us, I suggested that we should sink a hearth and build a fire-place with a flue and regular chimney of mud outside; and, with the help of the veteran Slate, the work was executed so well that our tent was always warm and clear of smoke, while the edges of the hearth made comfortable seats by which we could toast our feet, and recline back luxuriously. Tomasson, our bawling mess-mate, was not worth his salt at any work except legitimate soldiering. He seemed to consider that, by dusting around like a clown at a pantomime, and giving us the honour of his company, he did enough for the general welfare. Armstrong and Story were sergeants; and, of course, their Mightinesses were exempt from doing more than stooping to praise! Dan, being in the leading-strings of Story, was not permitted to roam; therefore, when it came to a consideration of ways and means for improving our diet, it devolved upon Malone, Slate, and myself to exert ourselves for the mess.

The long halt at Cave City served to initiate me into the mysteries of foraging, which, in army-vocabulary, meant not only to steal from the enemy, but to exploit Secessionist sympathisers, and obtain for love and money some trifles to make life more enjoyable. Malone and Slate were very successful and clever in all sorts of ruses. I was envious of the praises given to them, and resolved to outdo them. What rackings of the brain I suffered, as I mentally revolved the methods to adopt! General Sidney Johnston gave not so much time to the study of inflicting defeat on the Yankees, as I gave to win glory from the mess by my exploits. Half-a-dozen times in December it had been my turn to forage, but, somehow, my return was not greeted with any rapturous applause. However, by Christmas Eve I had a fair knowledge of the country and the temper of the people about, and my mind was stored with information regarding Secessionists, Unionists, and lanes, and farms, to a radius of five miles around the camp. Just on the edge of my circle, there lay one fat farm towards Green River, the owner of which was a Yank, and his

---

fell mortally wounded. Again HMS and his comrades in the Sixth Arkansas watched the action, being held in reserve (*OR*, 7:19–20. See also Neal and Kremm, *Lion of the South*, 97–99).

neighbour told me he corresponded with the enemy. For a foot-soldier, the distance was somewhat far, but for a horseman, it was nothing.

The day before Christmas, through the assistance of a man named Tate, I had the promise of a mule; and having obtained the countersign from Armstrong, I set out, as soon as it was dark, to levy a contribution on the Unionist farmer. It was about ten o'clock by the time I reached the place. Tying my mule in the angle of a fence, I climbed over, and explored the grounds. In crossing a field, I came to half-a-dozen low mounds, which I was certain contained stores of potatoes, or something of the kind. I burrowed into the side of one of them with my bayonet, and presently I smelled apples. These were even better than potatoes, for they would do splendidly for dumplings. I half-filled a sack with them. After burrowing into two or three others, I came to one which contained the winter store of potatoes, and I soon raked out enough to make a load. I hurried with my booty to my mule, and secured it on the mule.

Then, thinking that a goose, or even a duck or a fowl or two, would make our Christmas dinner complete, I was tempted to make a quest for them, anticipating, as I crept towards the farm, the glory I should receive from my mess. I reached the out-houses with every faculty strained, and I soon had the pleasure of wringing the neck of a goose, a duck, and two fowls.

I ought to have had the discretion to retire now, but the ambition to extinguish Malone and Slate, to see the grin of admiration on Armstrong's face, and Newton Story open his eyes, and Tomasson compelled to pay homage to worth, left me still dissatisfied; and just then scenting a hog-pen, I quietly moved towards it. By the light of a feeble moon I worked into the piggies' home, and there, cuddled about the hams of their mother, I saw the pinky forms of three or four plump shoats. Aye, a tender shoat, roasted brown and crisp, would be the crown of a Christmas dinner! I bounded lightly as a lean fox into the sty, snatched a young porkling up by the heels, creating a terrifying clamour by the act. We were all alarmed, the mother hoarsely grunted, the piggies squealed in frightful chorus, the innocent rent the midnight air with his cries; but, determined not to lose my prize, I scrambled over, ended its fears and struggles by one fierce slash, dumped the carcase into the sack, and then hastened away. Lights were visible in the farm-house, doors slammed, and by a broad beam of light I saw a man in the doorway with a gun in his hand. A second later a shower of pellets whistled about me, fortunately without harm, which sent me tearing madly towards my mule. In a few minutes, bathed in perspiration, I was astride of my mule, with my sack of dead meat in front of me, and potatoes and apples thumping the sides of my animal as I rode away towards camp.

Long before dawn, I made my triumphant appearance in front of my tent, and was rewarded by every member of the mess with the most grateful acknowledgements. The Christmas dinner was a splendid success, and over twenty invited guests sat down to it, and praises were on every lip; but without the apple dumplings and fritters it would not have been complete to us youngsters. Secretly, I was persuaded that it was as wrong to rob a poor Unionist as a Secessionist; but the word "foraging," which, by general consent, was bestowed on such deeds, mollified my scruples. Foragers were sent out by the authorities every other day, and even authorised to seize supplies by force; and, according to the military education I was receiving, I did not appear to be so very wicked as my conscience was inclined to make me out to be.

When I set out foraging in the daytime I was amply furnished with funds, and sought some fraternal "Secesh." Towards Green River, beyond the pickets, an old Secessionist lady and I became great friends, trusting one another without reservation. I would give her ten dollars at a time to invest in eggs, butter, and fowls and she would trust me with bowls, tins, and linen, to take the articles to camp. The old lady was wont to bless my "honest face" and to be emotional, as I told her of the sufferings of my fellow "Dixies" at camp, out in the snow and wintry gale. Her large faith in me, and her good heart, made me so scrupulous that I ran many risks to restore her property to her. Her features and widowed condition, the sight of her dairy utensils, clean, and smelling of laitage,[27] cream, and cheese, revived pleasing recollections of kine[28] and their night-stalls, and led on to Aunt Mary and her chimney-side; from that moment, I was her most devoted admirer. Through her favouritism for me, our mess was often able to lend a pound of fresh butter and a dozen eggs to the officers' mess.

One of the most singular characteristics of my comrades was their readiness to take offence at any reflection on their veracity or personal

---

27. French term for dairy products.
28. "Kine" is the archaic double plural of cow.

honour, and the most certain provocation of fury was to give anyone the lie. They could stand the most vulgar horse-play, sarcastic badinage, and cutting jokes, with good-humour; but, if that unhappy word escaped one in heat, or playful malice, it acted on their nerves as a red rag is said to do on a mad bull. The glory of a native Southerner consists in being reputed brave, truth-telling, and reverent towards women. On such subjects, no joking was permissible. He who ventured to cast a doubt upon either was liable to be called upon at an instant to withdraw it; and, if an angry tone made the doubter writhe, and indisposed to submit, there was sure to be a scene. To withdraw a word at an imperious command was to confess oneself inferior in courage to him who challenged; and, as all prided themselves on being of equal rank, and similarly endowed with the best qualities of manhood, I never met one who was morally brave enough to confess his fault and apologise, unless he was compelled by overwhelming odds.

During that winter I absorbed so many of these "chivalrous" ideas that I was in a fair way of becoming as great a fire-eater as any son of the South. Had it not been for Newton Story and Armstrong, who knew intuitively when to interpose their authority, Tomasson's rudeness, which flared me up many a time, would, I am sure, have been followed by deplorable consequences. There was young Dan also; he was often in a wrangling mood, and by his over-insistent glorifications of Southern chivalry brought us within a hair's breadth triggers.

The tedium of camp-life at Cave City was relieved by outbreaks of this kind, for, when we were not required to exhibit our courage against the common foe, the spirit of mischief found it an easy task to influence our susceptiveness when discussing such dear and near matters as valour, chastity, honour, and chivalry, the four chiefest virtues of the South. It is not an easy task to identify myself in the sunken hearth of the tent at Cave City, talking grandly upon such themes; but several scenes recur to the mind, and compel me to the humiliating confession that it *was* I.

This life did not tend to awaken spiritual thoughts, or religious observations. When, after a long lapse from piety, I strove to correct my erring disposition with the aid of prayer, how very faint-hearted I felt! I shrank from the least allusion to any goody-goodiness manifested; I became shame-faced if I was accused of being pious; the Bible was only opened by stealth; and I was as ready to deny that I prayed, as Peter was to deny Christ. A word or act of my neighbour became as perilous to my spiritual feelings as a gust of east wind is to a sufferer from Influenza. Every hour brought its obstacle; but I came, by degrees, to realise that, just as one must concentrate his reasoning faculties for the solution of a problem, I must, if I hoped to win in the great fight, summon every good thought to my assistance, and resolutely banish all false pride.

But these were not my worst faults. Tomasson's mad humour was as infectious as Dan's dissertations upon Southern chivalry. Indoors he was jestive, amusing, vulgarly-entertaining; outdoors, he made us all join him in uproarious laughter. The prank of a mule, the sight of a tall hat, the apparition of a black coat, a child, a woman, a duel between two cocks, a culprit undergoing penance, it mattered not what, tickled his humorous nerve, and instigated him to bawl, and yell, and break out into explosions of laughter; and whether we laughed at him, or at that which had caught his fancy, in a second we had joined in the yelling, the company became smitten with it, then the regiment, and, finally, the army, was convulsed in idiotic cachinnations. I really blushed at the follies that people like Tomasson often led us into; but, after all, these occasional bursts of jolly imbecility were only a way these free-born natures took to express their animal discontent and mild melancholy, under the humiliating circumstances of that crude period. It was really pathetic, after a mild paroxysm of this kind, to hear them sigh, and turn to each other and ask, "Who would sell a farm to become a soldier?"

From the day when personal decoration was not expected from the private soldiers, and we learned that endurance was more esteemed than comeliness, a steady deterioration in our appearance took place. We allowed weeks to pass by without a bath; our hair was mown, not cut, making a comb unnecessary; a bottle of water sufficed for ablution, a pocket-handkerchief, or the sleeve of our jacket, served for a towel; a dab of bacon-fat was all that was needed for our boots; our dingy grey uniforms required no brushing. Soldiering, as practised in time of war, was most demoralising in many ways; for the conflict against hunger, fatigue, cold, and exposure, exhausted the energies and strength of each individual.

By February, 1862, we had learned the trade of war tolerably well, and were rich in "wrinkles"; for no teacher is so thorough as necessity. We were no longer harrowed by the scarcity of comforts, and the climate, with its fickleness and inclemency, we proudly disregarded. Whether it rained, sleeted, or snowed, or the keen frost bit through to the marrow, mattered as little to us as it did to the military geniuses who expected raw soldiers to thrive on this Spartan training. To perfect content with our lot we could not hope to attain, so long as we retained each our spiritual individualities, and remembered what we had enjoyed in times gone-by; but, after a course of due seasoning, the worst ills only provoked a temporary ill-humour; while our susceptibility to fun so sweetened our life that there was scarcely anything in our lives but conduced to a laugh and prompted a jest.

The fall of Forts Henry and Donelson, on the 6th and 16th February, 1862, required our instant evacuation of Cave City and Bowling Green, to Nashville, lest we should be cut off by the Union advance up the Cumberland and Tennessee Rivers behind us. We were therefore obliged to march through the snow to the rear of Bowling Green, where we were packed into the cars and speedily taken to Nashville, arriving there on the 20th February. Thence, after a couple of days, we were marched towards the South, via Murfreesboro, Tullahoma, Athens, and Decatur, a march of two hundred and fifty miles. At the latter place we took the cars again, and were transported to Corinth, where we arrived on the 25th March.[29] Here it leaked out that a surprise was intended against our army, by the conqueror of Donelson, who had landed from the Tennessee River near Shiloh, some twenty-four miles away from us. Brigades and regiments were daily arriving, belonging to the divisions of Generals [Charles] Clark, [Benjamin F.] Cheatham, Bragg, [Jones M.] Withers, and [John C.] Breckenridge, which were finally formed into three army corps, under the inspection commands of [Leonidas] Polk, Braxton Bragg, and Hardee, and were now united under the commands of Generals Albert Sidney Johnston, and P. G. T. Beauregard.[30]

29. For an account of the movement of Hardee's and Hindman's men during the disastrous month of February 1862, see Nathaniel C. Hughes, Jr., *General William J. Hardee: Old Reliable* (Baton Rouge: Louisiana State University Press, 1965), 89–98.

30. Daniel Ruggles also commanded a division. Bragg and Breckinridge, however, commanded corps at Shiloh. The spelling of Breckinridge's name has been corrected in the text. For the complete order of the Battle at Shiloh, see Wiley Sword, *Shiloh: Bloody April* (Dayton, Ohio: Morningside Bookshop, 1983), 447–59.

6

Shiloh

On April 2, 1862, we received orders to prepare three days' cooked rations. Through some misunderstanding, we did not set out until the 4th; and, on the morning of that day, the 6th Arkansas Regiment of Hindman's brigade, Hardee's corps, marched from Corinth to take part in one of the bloodiest battles of the West.[1] We left knapsacks and tents behind us. After two days of marching, and two nights of bivouacking and living on cold rations, our spirits were not so buoyant at dawn of Sunday, the 6th April, as they ought to have been for the serious task before us. Many wished, like myself, that we had not been required to undergo this discomfort before being precipitated into the midst of a great battle.

Military science, with all due respect to our generals, was not at that time what it is now. Our military leaders were well acquainted with the science of war, and, in the gross fashion prevailing, paid proper attention to the commissariat. Every soldier had his lawful allowance of raw provender dealt out to him; but, as to its uses and effects, no one seemed to be concerned. Future commanding generals will doubtless

---

1. Maj. Gen. William J. Hardee's Third Corps consisted of the brigades of Hindman, Patrick R. Cleburne, and Sterling A. M. Wood. Hindman's brigade at Shiloh would be commanded by Col. R. G. Shaver while Hindman himself acted as a division commander, leading his own and Wood's brigades. Hindman's brigade consisted of the Second Arkansas Infantry (Col. Daniel C. Govan), Sixth Arkansas Infantry (Col. Alexander T. Hawthorn), Seventh Arkansas Infantry (Lt. Col. John M. Dean), Third Confederate Infantry (Col. John S. Marmaduke), and Swett's Mississippi Battery (Capt. Charles Swett) (*OR*, 52[1]:28; 10[1]:383).

remedy this, and when they meditate staking their cause and reputation on a battle, they will, like the woodman about to do good day's work at cutting timber, see that their instruments are in the best possible state for their purpose.

Generals Johnston and Beauregard proposed to hurl into the Tennessee River an army of nearly 50,000 rested and well-fed troops, by means of 40,000 soldiers, who, for two days, had subsisted on sodden biscuit and raw bacon, who had been exposed for two nights to rain and dew, and had marched twenty-three miles![2] Considering that at least a fourth of our force were lads under twenty, and that such a strenuous task was before them, it suggests itself to me that the omission to take the physical powers of those youths into their calculation had as much to do with the failure of the project as the obstinate courage of General Grant's troops. According to authority, the actual number of the forces about to be opposed to each other was 39,630 Confederates against 49,232 Federals.[3] Our generals expected the arrival of General Van Dorn, with 20,000 troops, who failed to make their appearance; but, close at hand to Grant, was General Buell's force of 20,000, who, opportunely for Grant, arrived just at the close of the day's battle.

At four o'clock in the morning, we rose from our damp bivouac, and, after a hasty refreshment, were formed into line. We stood in rank for half an hour or so, while the military dispositions were being completed along the three-mile front. Our brigade formed the centre; Cleburne's and Gladden's brigades were on our respective flanks.[4]

Day broke with every promise of a fine day. Next to me, on my right, was a boy of seventeen, Henry Parker. I remember it because, while we stood-at-ease, he drew my attention to some violets at his feet, and said, "It would be a good idea to put a few into my cap. Perhaps the Yanks won't shoot me if they see me wearing such flowers, for they are a sign of peace." "Capital," said I, "I will do the same." We plucked a bunch,

2. Shiloh historian Larry Daniel puts USA strength at 48,894 (April 6), 66,812 (April 7); CSA strength at 44,699 (Larry J. Daniel, *Shiloh: The Battle that Changed the Civil War* [New York: Simon & Schuster, 1997], 322).

3. HMS's "authority" appears to have been the *Official Records*, 10(1):112–13, 398–99.

4. Patrick R. Cleburne's brigade initially formed on the left of Hindman's two brigades with Adley H. Gladden's brigade on Hindman's right. Within Hindman's command, immediately to the left of HMS's brigade, was Sterling A. M. Wood's Alabama-Arkansas-Tennessee brigade (Hughes, *Hardee*, 105).

and arranged the violets in our caps. The men in the ranks laughed at our proceedings, and had not the enemy been so near, their merry mood might have been communicated to the army.

We loaded our muskets, and arranged our cartridge-pouches ready for use. Our weapons were the obsolete flint-locks,[5] and the ammunition was rolled in cartridge-paper, which contained powder, a round ball, and three buckshot. When we loaded we had to tear the paper with our teeth, empty a little powder into the pan, lock it, empty the rest of the powder into the barrel, press paper and ball into the muzzle, and ram home. Then the Orderly-sergeant called the roll, and we knew that the Dixie Greys were present to a man. Soon after, there was a commotion, and we dressed up smartly. A young Aide galloped along our front, gave some instructions to the Brigadier Hindman, who confided the same to his Colonels, and presently we swayed forward in line, with shouldered arms.[6] Newton Story, big, broad, and straight, bore our company-banner of gay silk, at which the ladies of our neighbourhood had laboured.[7]

As we tramped solemnly and silently through the thin forest, and over its grass, still in its withered and wintry hue, I noticed that the sun was not far from appearing, that our regiment was keeping its formation admirably, that the woods would have been a grand place for a picnic; and I thought it strange that a Sunday should have been chosen to disturb the holy calm of those woods.

Before we had gone five hundred paces, our serenity was disturbed by some desultory firing in front. It was then a quarter-past five. "They

5. DTS's note: "Beauregard (*Military Operations*, vol. i, p. 300), writing of the battlefield of Shiloh, says, 'One cheering feature, however, was the strewing of old flint-locks and double-barrelled shot-guns, exchanged for the Enfield and Minie rifles abandoned by the enemy.' " Col. Robert G. Shaver, brigade commander, remarked: "The Seventh and Sixth Arkansas labored under great disadvantage during the engagement; being armed with flint and steel muskets, they were rarely able to do any execution, the enemy always endeavoring to fight us at long range. It is with great difficulty that men can be made to stand their ground when they are suffering from the fire of their adversaries and are in possession of the knowledge that from the inefficiency of their pieces they are doing no execution in return" (Stanley, *Autobiography*, 187n; *OR*, 10[1]:575–76).

6. Corps commander Hardee had created a "provisional division" consisting of the brigades of Robert G. Shaver and Sterling A. M. Wood, commanded by Hindman (Daniel, *Shiloh*, 149).

7. Hindman's men, as did the others of Hardee's corps, carried into battle "a blue flag bordered with white and bearing a white 'silver moon' " in the center (ibid., 95).

are at it already," we whispered to each other. "Stand by, gentle-men,"—for we were all gentlemen volunteers at this time,—said our Captain, S. G. Smith.[8] Our steps became unconsciously brisker, and alertness was noticeable in everybody. The firing continued at intervals, deliberate and scattered, as at target-practice. We drew nearer to the firing, and soon a sharper rattling of musketry was heard. "That is the enemy waking up," we said. Within a few minutes, there was another explosive burst of musketry, the air was pierced by many missiles, which hummed and pinged sharply by our ears, pattered through the tree-tops, and brought twigs and leaves down on us. "Those are bullets," Henry whispered with awe.

At two hundred yards further, a dreadful roar of musketry broke out from a regiment adjoining ours. It was followed by another further off, and the sound had scarcely died away when regiment after regiment blazed away and made a continuous roll of sound. "We are in for it now," said Henry; but as yet we had seen nothing, though our ears were tingling under the animated volleys.

"Forward, gentlemen, make ready!" urged Captain Smith. In re-sponse, we surged forward, for the first time marring the alignment. We trampled recklessly over the grass and young sprouts. Beams of sunlight stole athwart our course. The sun was up above the horizon. Just then we came to a bit of packland, and overtook our skirmishers, who had been engaged in exploring our front.[9] We passed beyond them. Noth-ing now stood between us and the enemy.

"There they are!" was no sooner uttered, than we cracked into them with levelled muskets. "Aim low, men!" commanded Captain Smith. I tried hard to see some living thing to shoot at, for it appeared absurd to be blazing away at shadows. But, still advancing, firing as we moved, I, at last, saw a row of little globes of pearly smoke streaked with crimson, breaking-out, with spurtive quickness, from a long line of bluey figures in front; and, simultaneously, there broke upon our ears an appalling

8. "L. G. Smith" is an obvious error that has been corrected by the editor. In the previous chapter Captain S. G. Smith had been correctly identified by editor DTS.

9. HMS's account is consistent with that of Colonel Shaver who reported a steady advance against "no very persistent resistance" until beginning the attack upon the sec-ond ridge. Sword maintains that Shaver had shown his inexperience by halting his brigade and pushing out skirmishers. The delay enabled the enemy to organize a line of battle that led to the heavy fire described by HMS (*OR*, 10[1]:573; Sword, *Shiloh*, 151–53).

Stanley at age twenty

crash of sound, the series of fusillades following one another with star-
tling suddenness, which suggested to my somewhat moidered sense a
mountain upheaved, with huge rocks tumbling and thundering down a
slope, and the echoes rumbling and receding through space. Again and
again, these loud and quick explosions were repeated, seemingly with
increased violence, until they rose to the highest pitch of fury, and in
unbroken continuity. All the world seemed involved in one tremendous
ruin!

This was how the conflict was ushered in—as it affected me. I looked
around to see the effect on others, or whether I was singular in my emotions, and was glad to notice that each was possessed with his own
thoughts. All were pale, solemn, and absorbed; but, beyond that, it was
impossible for me to discover what they thought of it; but, by transmission of sympathy, I felt that they would gladly prefer to be elsewhere,
though the law of the inevitable kept them in line to meet their destiny.
It might be mentioned, however, that at no time were we more instinctively inclined to obey the voice of command. We had no individuality
at this moment, but all motions and thoughts were surrendered to the

unseen influence which directed our movements. Probably few bothered their minds with self-questionings as to the issue to themselves. That properly belongs to other moments, to the night, to the interval between waking and sleeping, to the first moments of the dawn—not when every nerve is tense, and the spirit is at the highest pitch of action. Though one's senses were preternaturally acute, and engaged with their impressions, we plied our arms, loaded, and fired, with such nervous haste as though it depended on each of us how soon this fiendish uproar would be hushed. My nerves tingled, my pulses beat double-quick, my heart throbbed loudly, and almost painfully; but, amid all the excitement, my thoughts, swift as the flash of lightning, took all sound, and sight, and self, into their purview. I listened to the battle raging far away on the flanks, to the thunder in front, to the various sounds made by the leaden storm. I was angry with my rear rank, because he made my eyes smart with the powder of his musket; and I felt like cuffing him for deafening my ears![10] I knew how Captain Smith and Lieutenant Mason looked, how bravely the "Dixie Greys" banner ruffled over Newton Story's head, and that all hands were behaving as though they knew how long all this would last. Back to myself my thoughts came, and, with the whirring bullet, they fled to the blue-bloused ranks afront. They dwelt on their movements, and read their temper, as I should read time by a clock. Through the lurid haze the contours of their pink faces could not be seen, but their gappy, hesitating, incoherent, and sensitive line revealed their mood clearly.

We continued advancing, step by step, loading and firing as we went. To every forward step, they took a backward move, loading and firing as they slowly withdrew. Twenty thousand muskets were being fired at this stage, but, though accuracy of aim was impossible, owing to our labouring hearts, and the jarring and excitement, many bullets found their destined billets on both sides.

After a steady exchange of musketry, which lasted some time, we heard the order: "Fix Bayonets! On the double-quick!" in tones that

10. A similar experience was recorded by another Arkansas private six months earlier at the Battle of Belmont. Phil Stephenson complained: "Barney Finigan, a huge lumbering Irishman, was just behind me in the rear rank. Presently I felt my hat blown off. Barney put his gun deliberately to the back of my head. Garland Webb knocked the gun up with his sword, and the bullet had blown my hat off!" (Stephenson, *Civil War Memoir*, 30).

thrilled us. There was a simultaneous bound forward, each soul doing his best for the emergency. The Federals appeared inclined to await us; but, at this juncture, our men raised a yell, thousands responded to it, and burst out into the wildest yelling it has ever been my lot to hear. It drove all sanity and order from among us. It served the double purpose of relieving pent-up feelings, and transmitting encouragement along the attacking line. I rejoiced in the shouting like the rest. It reminded me that there were about four hundred companies like the Dixie Greys, who shared our feelings. Most of us, engrossed with the musket-work, had forgotten the fact; but the wave after wave of human voices, louder than all other battle-sounds together, penetrated to every sense, and stimulated our energies to the utmost.

"They fly!" was echoed from lip to lip. It accelerated our pace, and filled us with a noble rage. Then I knew what the Berserker passion was![11] It deluged us with rapture, and transfigured each Southerner into an exulting victor. At such a moment, nothing could have halted us.

Those savage yells, and the sight of thousands of racing figures coming towards them, discomfited the blue-coats; and when we arrived upon the place where they had stood, they had vanished. Then we caught sight of their beautiful array of tents, before which they had made their stand, after being roused from their Sunday-morning sleep, and huddled into line, at hearing their pickets challenge our skirmishers. The half-dressed dead and wounded showed what a surprise our attack had been. We drew up in the enemy's camp, panting and breathing hard. Some precious minutes were thus lost in recovering our breaths, indulging our curiosity, and re-forming our line. Signs of a hasty rouse to the battle were abundant. Military equipments, uniform-coats, half-packed knapsacks, bedding, of a new and superior quality, littered the company streets.

Meantime, a series of other camps lay behind the first array of tents. The resistance we had met, though comparatively brief, enabled the brigades in rear of the advance camp to recover from the shock of the surprise; but our delay had not been long enough to give them time to form in proper order of battle. There were wide gaps between their di-

---

11. HMS refers to the mythical Scandinavian being, at once savage, irrational, and tempestuous—"hence any man with the fighting fever on him" (William R. Benét, *The Reader's Encyclopedia* [New York: Thomas Y. Crowell, 1948], 100).

visions, into which the quick-flowing tide of elated Southerners entered, and compelled them to fall back lest they should be surrounded. Prentiss's brigade, despite their most desperate efforts, were thus hemmed in on all sides, and were made prisoners.[12]

I had a momentary impression that, with the capture of the first camp, the battle was well-nigh over; but, in fact, it was only a brief prologue of the long and exhaustive series of struggles which took place that day.

Continuing our advance, we came in view of the tops of another mass of white tents, and, almost at the same time, were met by a furious storm of bullets, poured on us from a long line of blue-coats, whose attitude of assurance proved to us that we should have tough work here. But we were so much heartened by our first success that it would have required a good deal to have halted our advance for long. Their opportunity for making a full impression on us came with terrific suddenness. The world seemed bursting into fragments. Cannon and musket, shell and bullet, lent their several intensities to the distracting uproar. If I had not a fraction of an ear, and an eye inclined toward my Captain and Company, I had been spell-bound by the energies now opposed to us. I likened the cannon, with their deep bass, to the roaring of a great herd of lions; the ripping, cracking musketry, to the incessant yapping of terriers; the windy whisk of shells, and zipping of minie bullets, to the swoop of eagles, and the buzz of angry wasps. All the opposing armies of Grey and Blue fiercely blazed at each other.

After being exposed for a few seconds to this fearful downpour, we heard the order to "Lie down, men, and continue your firing!" Before me was a prostrate tree, about fifteen inches in diameter, with a narrow strip of light between it and the ground. Behind this shelter a dozen of us flung ourselves. The security it appeared to offer restored me to my individuality. We could fight, and think, and observe, better than out in the open. But it was a terrible period! How the cannon bellowed, and their shells plunged and bounded, and flew with screeching hisses over us! Their sharp rending explosions and hurtling fragments made us shrink and cower, despite our utmost efforts to be cool and collected. I

12. HMS mistakes the camp. Benjamin M. Prentiss's camp(s) fell only after the very heavy fighting that was to follow. Brigadier General Prentiss, moreover, commanded not a brigade but the Union Sixth Division.

marvelled as I heard the unintermitting patter, snip, thud, and hum of the bullets, how anyone could live under this raining death. I could hear the balls beating a merciless tattoo on the outer surface of the log, pinging vivaciously as they flew off at a tangent from it, and thudding into something or other, at the rate of a hundred a second. One, here and there, found its way under the log, and buried itself in a comrade's body. One man raised his chest, as if to yawn, and jostled me. I turned to him, and saw that a bullet had gored his whole face, and penetrated into his chest. Another ball struck a man a deadly rap on the head, and he turned on his back and showed his ghastly white face to the sky.

"It's getting too warm, boys!" cried a soldier, and he uttered a vehement curse upon keeping soldiers hugging the ground until every ounce of courage was chilled. He lifted his head a little too high, and a bullet skimmed over the top of the log and hit him fairly in the centre of his forehead, and he fell heavily on his face. But his thought had been instantaneously general; and the officers, with one voice, ordered the charge; and cries of "Forward, forward!" raised us, as with a spring, to our feet, and changed the complexion of our feelings. The pulse of action beat feverishly once more; and, though overhead was crowded with peril, we were unable to give it so much attention as when we lay stretched on the ground.

Just as we bent our bodies for the onset, a boy's voice cried out, "Oh, stop, *please* stop a bit, I have been hurt, and can't move!" I turned to look, and saw Henry Parker, standing on one leg, and dolefully regarding his smashed foot.[13] In another second, we were striding impetuously towards the enemy, vigorously plying our muskets, stopping only to prime the pan and ram the load down, when, with a spring or two, we would fetch up with the front, aim and fire.

Our progress was not so continuously rapid as we desired, for the blues were obdurate; but at this moment we were gladdened at the sight of a battery galloping to our assistance.[14] It was time for nerve-shaking

13. Pvt. Henry D. Parker, age eighteen, had enlisted with HMS. Probably permanently disabled, he would be discharged from the army on April 10, 1862, "on acc. of wound received at the Battle of Shiloh" (H. D. Parker CSR).

14. "Captain Charles Swett's Warren (Mississippi) Light Artillery from Vicksburg galloped up and unlimbered their six pieces to the right of Shaver's men. Their destructive fire ripped through Sibley tents, ploughed up the ground, tore large limbs from trees. Being within rifle range, the gunners soon began to take casualties. Hardee directed Hindman to save the battery" (Daniel, *Shiloh*, 151).

cannon to speak. After two rounds of shell and canister, we felt the pressure on us slightly relaxed; but we were still somewhat sluggish in disposition, though the officers' voices rang out imperiously. Newton Story at this juncture strode forward rapidly with the Dixies' banner, until he was quite sixty yards ahead of the foremost. Finding himself alone, he halted; and turning to us smilingly, said, "Why don't you come on, boys? You see there is no danger!" His smile and words acted on us like magic. We raised the yell, and sprang lightly and hopefully towards him. "Let's give them hell, boys!" said one. "Plug them plum-centre, every time!"

It was all very encouraging, for the yelling and shouting were taken up by thousands. "Forward, forward; don't give them breathing time!" was cried. We instinctively obeyed, and soon came in clear view of the blue-coats, who were scornfully unconcerned at first; but, seeing the leaping tide of men coming on at a tremendous pace, their front dissolved, and they fled in double-quick retreat. Again we felt the "glorious joy of heroes." It carried us on exultantly, rejoicing in the spirit which recognises nothing but the prey. We were no longer an army of soldiers, but so many school-boys racing in which length of legs, wind, and condition tell.

We gained the second line of camps, continued the rush through them, and clean beyond. It was now about ten o'clock. My physical powers were quite exhausted, and, to add to my discomfiture, something struck me on my belt-clasp, and tumbled me headlong to the ground.

I could not have been many minutes prostrated before I recovered from the shock of the blow and fall, to find my clasp deeply dented and cracked. My company was not in sight. I was grateful for the rest, and crawled feebly to a tree, and plunging my hand into my haversack, ate ravenously. Within half an hour, feeling renovated, I struck north in the direction which my regiment had taken, over a ground strewn with bodies and the débris of war.

The desperate character of this day's battle was now brought home to my mind in all its awful reality. While in the tumultuous advance, and occupied with a myriad of exciting incidents, it was only at brief intervals that I was conscious of wounds being given and received; but now, in the trail of pursuers and pursued, the ghastly relics appalled every sense. I felt curious as to who the fallen Greys were, and moved to one stretched straight out. It was the body of a stout English Sergeant of a neighbouring company, the members of which hailed principally from the Washita Valley.[15] At the crossing of the Arkansas River this plump, ruddy-faced man had been conspicuous for his complexion, jovial features and good-humour, and had been nicknamed "John Bull." He was now lifeless, and lay with his eyes wide open, regardless of the scorching sun, and the tempestuous cannonade which sounded through the forest, and the musketry that crackled incessantly along the front.

Close by him was a young Lieutenant, who, judging by the new gloss on his uniform, must have been some father's darling. A clean bullet-hole through the centre of his fore-head had instantly ended his career. A little further were some twenty bodies, lying in various postures, each by its own pool of viscous blood, which emitted a peculiar scent, which was new to me, but which I have since learned is inseparable from a battle-field. Beyond these, a still larger group lay, body overlying body, knees crooked, arms erect, or wide-stretched and rigid, according as the last spasm overtook them. The company opposed to them must have shot straight.

Other details of that ghastly trail formed a mass of horrors that will always be remembered at the mention of Shiloh. I can never forget the impression those wide-open dead eyes made on me. Each seemed to be starting out of its socket, with a look similar to the fixed wondering gaze of an infant, as though the dying had viewed something appalling at the last moment. "Can it be," I asked myself, "that at the last glance they saw their own retreating souls, and wondered why their caskets were left behind, like offal?" My surprise was that the form we made so much of, and that nothing was too good for, should now be mutilated, hacked, and outraged; and that the life, hitherto guarded as a sacred thing, and protected by the Constitution, Law, Ministers of Justice, Police, should, of a sudden,—at least, before I can realise it,—be given up to death!

An object once seen, if it has affected my imagination, remains indelibly fixed in my memory; and, among many other scenes with which it is now crowded, I cannot forget that half-mile square of woodland, lighted brightly by the sun, and littered by the forms of about a thousand dead and wounded men, and by horses, and military equipments.

15. HMS refers to Company K, the Ouachita Grays.

It formed a picture that may always be reproduced with almost absolute fidelity. For it was the first Field of Glory I had seen in my May of life, and the first time that Glory sickened me with its repulsive aspect, and made me suspect it was all a glittering lie. In my imagination, I saw more than it was my fate to see with my eyes, for, under a flag of truce, I saw the bearers pick up the dead from the field, and lay them in long rows beside a wide trench; I saw them laid, one by one, close together at the bottom,—thankless victims of a perished cause, and all their individual hopes, pride, honour, names, buried under oblivious earth.

My thoughts reverted to the time when these festering bodies were idolized objects of their mothers' passionate love, their fathers standing by, half-fearing to touch the fragile little things, and the wings of civil law out-spread to protect parents and children in their family loves, their coming and going followed with pride and praise, and the blessing of the Almighty over-shadowing all. Then, as they were nearing manhood, through some strange warp of Society, men in authority summoned them from school and shop, field and farm, to meet in the woods on a Sunday morning for mutual butchery with the deadliest instruments ever invented, Civil Law, Religion, and Morality complaisantly standing aside, while 90,000 young men, who had been preached and moralized to, for years, were let loose to engage in the carnival of slaughter.

Only yesterday, they professed to shudder at the word "Murder." To-day, by a strange twist in human nature, they lusted to kill, and were hounded on in the work of destruction by their pastors, elders, mothers, and sisters. Oh, for once, I was beginning to know the real truth! Man was born for slaughter! All the pains taken to soothe his savage heart were unavailing! Holy words and heavenly hopes had no lasting effect on his bestial nature, for, when once provoked, how swiftly he flung aside the sweet hope of Heaven, and the dread of Hell, with which he amused himself in time of ease!

As I moved, horror-stricken, through the fearful shambles, where the dead lay as thick as the sleepers in a London park on a Bank Holiday, I was unable to resist the belief that my education had been in abstract things, which had no relation to our animal existence. For, if human life is so disparaged, what has it to do with such high subjects as God, Heaven, and Immortality? And to think how devotional men and women pretended to be, on a Sunday! Oh, cunning, cruel man! He knew that the sum of all real knowledge and effort was to know how to kill and mangle his brothers, as we were doing to-day! Reflecting on my own emotions, I wondered if other youths would feel that they had been deluded like myself with man's fine polemics and names of things, which vanished with the reality.

A multitude of angry thoughts surged through me, which I cannot describe in detail, but they amounted to this, that a cruel deception had been practised on my blank ignorance, that my atom of imagination and feeling had been darkened, and that man was a portentous creature from which I recoiled with terror and pity. He was certainly terrible and hard, but was no more to me now than a two-legged beast; he was cunning beyond finding out, but his morality was only a mask for his wolfish heart! Thus, scoffing and railing at my infatuation for moral excellence as practised by humanity, I sought to join my company and regiment.

The battle-field maintained the same character of undulated woodland, being, in general, low ridges separated by broad depressions, which sunk occasionally into ravines of respectable depth. At various places, wide clearings had been made; and I came across a damp bottom or two covered with shrubs. For a defensive force there were several positions that were admirable as rallying-points, and it is perhaps owing to these, and the undoubted courage exhibited by the Federal troops, that the battle was so protracted. Though our attack had been a surprise, it was certain that they fought as though they were resolved to deny it; and, as the ground to be won from the enemy was nearly five miles in depth, and every half mile or so they stood and obstinately contested it, all the honours of the day were not to be with us.

I overtook my regiment about one o'clock, and found that it was engaged in one of these occasional spurts of fury. The enemy resolutely maintained their ground, and our side was preparing for another assault. The firing was alternately brisk and slack. We lay down, and availed ourselves of trees, logs, and hollows, and annoyed their upstanding ranks; battery pounded battery, and, meanwhile, we hugged our resting-places closely. Of a sudden, we rose and raced towards the position, and took it by sheer weight and impetuosity, as we had done before. About three o'clock, the battle grew very hot. The enemy appeared to be more concentrated, and immovably sullen.[16] Both sides fired better as they grew more accustomed to the din; but, with assistance from the reserves, we were continually pressing them towards the river Tennessee, without ever retreating an inch.

About this time, the enemy were assisted by the gun-boats, which hurled their enormous projectiles far beyond us; but, though they made great havoc among the trees, and created terror, they did comparatively little damage to those in close touch with the enemy.[17]

The screaming of the big shells, when they first began to sail over our heads, had the effect of reducing our fire; for they were as fascinating as they were distracting. But we became used to them, and our attention was being claimed more in front. Our officers were more urgent; and, when we saw the growing dyke of white cloud that signalled the bullet-storm, we could not be indifferent to the more immediate danger. Dead bodies, wounded men writhing in agony, and assuming every distressful attitude, were frequent sights; but what made us heart-sick was to see, now and then, the well-groomed charger of an officer, with fine saddle, and scarlet and yellow-edged cloth, and brass-tipped holsters, or a stray cavalry or artillery horse, galloping between the lines, snorting with terror, while his entrails, soiled with dust, trailed behind him.

Our officers had continued to show the same alertness and vigour throughout the day; but, as it drew near four o'clock, though they strove to encourage and urge us on, they began to abate somewhat in their energy; and it was evident that the pluckiest of the men lacked the spontaneity and springing ardour which had distinguished them earlier in the day. Several of our company lagged wearily behind, and the remainder showed, by their drawn faces, the effects of their efforts. Yet, after a short rest, they were able to make splendid spurts. As for myself, I had only one wish, and that was for repose. The long-continued excitement, the successive tautening and relaxing of the nerves, the

16. HMS describes the attacks made by Shaver's brigade against the stubbornly held Union position at the Hornets' Nest (see Daniel, *Shiloh*, 212–14; Sword, *Shiloh*, 293–95; *OR*, 10[1]:578–79).

17. Sword contends that the fire from the gunboats compelled General Beauregard to halt the pursuit. " 'The victory is sufficiently complete,' " Beauregard observed, " 'it is needless to expose our men to the fire of the gunboats' " (Sword, *Shiloh*, 363, 366).

quenchless thirst, made more intense by the fumes of sulphurous powder, and the caking grime on the lips, caused by tearing the paper cartridges, and a ravening hunger, all combined, had reduced me to a walking automaton, and I earnestly wished that night would come, and stop all further effort.

Finally, about five o'clock, we assaulted and captured a large camp; after driving the enemy well away from it, the front line was as thin as that of a skirmishing body, and we were ordered to retire to the tents. There we hungrily sought after provisions, and I was lucky in finding a supply of biscuits and a canteen of excellent molasses, which gave great comfort to myself and friends. The plunder in the camp was abundant. There were bedding, clothing, and accoutrements without stint; but people were so exhausted they could do no more than idly turn the things over. Night soon fell, and only a few stray shots could now be heard, to remind us of the thrilling and horrid din of the day, excepting the huge bombs from the gun-boats, which, as we were not far from the blue-coats, discomfited only those in the rear. By eight o'clock, I was repeating my experiences in the region of dreams, indifferent to columbiads[18] and mortars,[19] and the torrential rain which, at midnight, increased the miseries of the wounded and tentless.

An hour before dawn, I awoke from a refreshing sleep; and, after a hearty replenishment of my vitals with biscuit and molasses, I conceived myself to be fresher than on Sunday morning. While awaiting daybreak, I gathered from other early risers their ideas in regard to the events of yesterday. They were under the impression that we had gained a great victory, though we had not, as we had anticipated, reached the Tennessee River. Van Dorn, with his expected reinforcements for us, was not likely to make his appearance for many days yet; and, if General Buell, with his 20,000 troops, had joined the enemy during the night, we had a bad day's work before us. We were short of provisions and ammunition, General Sidney Johnston, our chief Com-

18. HMS refers to the very large guns he had seen on the bluffs at Columbus. The "Lady Polk" is an outstanding example. The gunboats (*Tyler* and *Lexington*) lobbing shells at the sleeping Confederates, however, were armed with eight-inch shell guns (Hughes, *Battle of Belmont*, 62–63; Daniel, *Shiloh*, 72; Ulysses S. Grant, "The Battle of Shiloh," *Battles and Leaders of the Civil War* [*B&L*], 1:485).

19. "The Federal gunboats had been ordered to fire at short intervals throughout the night 'to keep the Confederates from sleeping or resting' " (Sword, *Shiloh*, 373–74).

mander, had been killed; but Beauregard was safe and unhurt, and, if Buell was absent, we would win the day.[20]

At daylight, I fell in with my Company, but there were only about fifty of the Dixies present. Almost immediately after, symptoms of the coming battle were manifest. Regiments were hurried into line, but, even to my inexperienced eyes, the troops were in ill-condition for repeating the efforts of Sunday. However, in brief time, in consequence of our pickets being driven in on us, we were moved forward in skirmishing order. With my musket on the trail I found myself in active motion, more active than otherwise I would have been, perhaps, because Captain Smith had said, "Now, Mr. Stanley, if you please, step briskly forward!" This singling-out of me wounded my *amour-propre*, and sent me forward like a rocket. In a short time, we met our opponents in the same formation as ourselves, and advancing most resolutely. We threw ourselves behind such trees as were near us, fired, loaded, and darted forward to another shelter. Presently, I found myself in an open, grassy space, with no convenient tree or stump near; but, seeing a shallow hollow some twenty paces ahead, I made a dash for it, and plied my musket with haste. I became so absorbed with some blue figures in front of me, that I did pay sufficient heed to my companion greys; the open space was too dangerous, perhaps, for their advance; for, had they emerged, I should have known they were pressing forward. Seeing my blues in about the same proportion, I assumed that the greys were keeping their position, and never once thought of retreat.[21] However, as, despite our firing, the blues were coming uncomfortably near, I rose from my hollow; but, to my speechless amazement, I found myself a solitary grey, in a line of blue skirmishers! My companions had retreated! The next I heard was, "Down with that gun, Secesh, or I'll drill a hole through you! Drop it, quick!"

Half a dozen of the enemy were covering me at the same instant, and

20. HMS reveals he is writing with the advantage of thirty years hindsight. Pvt. Henry Stanley, in all probability, knew nothing of Buell nor of Van Dorn.

21. For substantiating first-hand accounts by the commanders of the Second and Seventh Arkansas, see *OR*, 10(1):577, 579. The "wearied and almost famished men" of Hindman's brigade, reported Col. James T. Martin, attempted to attack on Monday morning, but were soon flanked and under a heavy cross-fire themselves. "Our cut-up and disorganized forces," as Martin called them, retired and established a new line that then broke (*OR*, 10[1]:579).

I dropped my weapon, incontinently. Two men sprang at my collar, and marched me, unresisting, into the ranks of the terrible Yankees. *I was a prisoner!*[22]

When the senses have been concentrated upon a specific object with the intensity which a battle compels, and are forcibly and suddenly veered about by another will, the immediate result is, at first, stupefying. Before my consciousness had returned to me, I was being propelled vigorously from behind, and I was in view of a long, swaying line of soldiers, who were marching to meet us with all the precision of drill, and with such a close front that a rabbit would have found it difficult to break through.[23] This sight restored me to all my faculties, and I remembered I was a Confederate, in misfortune, and that it behoved me to have some regard for my Uniform. I heard bursts of vituperation from several hoarse throats, which straightened my back and made me defiant.

"Where are you taking that fellow to? Drive a bayonet into the ———— ————! Let him drop where he is!" they cried by the dozen, with a German accent. They grew more excited as we drew nearer, and more men joined in the opprobrious chorus. Then a few dashed from the ranks, with levelled bayonets, to execute what appeared to be the general wish.

I looked into their faces, deformed with fear and fury, and I felt intolerable loathing for the wild-eyed brutes! Their eyes, projected and distended, appeared like spots of pale blue ink, in faces of dough! Reason had fled altogether from their features, and, to appeal for mercy to such blind, ferocious animalism would have been the height of absurdity, but I was absolutely indifferent as to what they might do with me now. Could I have multiplied myself into a thousand, such unintellectual-looking louts might have been brushed out of existence with ease—

22. Confederate records show HMS enlisting June 1, 1861, at age eighteen, and present until April 7, 1862, "missing since the Battle of Shiloh." As with the 1860 Arkansas census, HMS's CSR lists him as William H. Stanley, not Henry Stanley. Federal records at Camp Douglas, however, show him as H. Stanley.

23. Upon occasion the Confederates, with time on their hands and little in their stomachs, would organize rabbit hunts. One such hunt occurred in Columbus late in the fall. Pvt. Phil Stephenson reported the men formed into two great lines, armed themselves with "sticks and stones," and the lines advanced toward each other driving rabbits, "hundreds of them, nay thousands. The poor foolish timid things hardly knew which way to run, and were slaughtered wholesale" (Stephenson, *Civil War Memoir*, 44).

despite their numbers. They were apparently new troops, from such back-lands as were favoured by German immigrants; and, though of sturdy build, another such mass of savagery and stupidity could not have been found within the four corners of North America. How I wished I could return to the Confederates, and tell them what kind of people were opposing them!

Before their bayonets reached me, my two guards, who were ruddy-faced Ohioans, flung themselves before me, and, presenting their rifles, cried, "Here! stop that, you fellows! He is our prisoner!" A couple of officers were almost as quick as they, and flourished their swords; and, amid an expenditure of profanity, drove them quickly back into their ranks, cursing and blackguarding me in a manner truly American. A company opened its lines as we passed to the rear. Once through, I was comparatively safe from the Union troops, but not from the Confederate missiles, which were dropping about, and striking men, right and left.

Quickening our pace, we soon were beyond danger from my friends; after which, I looked about with interest at the forces that were marching to retrieve their shame of yesterday. The troops we saw belonged to Buell, who had crossed the Tennessee, and was now joined by Grant. They presented a brave, even imposing, sight; and, in their new uniforms, with glossy knapsacks, rubbers undimmed, brasses resplendent, they approached nearer to my idea of soldiers than our dingy grey troops. Much of this fine show and seeming steadiness was due to their newer equipments, and, as yet, unshaken nerves; but, though their movements were firm, they were languid, and lacked the élan, the bold confidence, of the Southerners. Given twenty-four hours' rest, and the enjoyment of cooked rations, I felt that the Confederates would have crumpled up the handsome Unionists within a brief time.

Though my eyes had abundant matter of interest within their range, my mind continually harked back to the miserable hollow which had disgraced me, and I kept wondering how it was that my fellow-skirmishers had so quickly disappeared. I was inclined to blame Captain Smith for urging me on, when, within a few minutes after, he must have withdrawn his men. But it was useless to trouble my mind with conjectures. I was a prisoner! Shameful position! What would become of my knapsack, and my little treasures,—letters, and souvenirs of my father? They were lost beyond recovery!

On the way, my guards and I had a discussion about our respective causes, and, though I could not admit it, there was much reason in what they said, and I marvelled that they could put their case so well. For, until now, I was under the impression that they were robbers who only sought to desolate the South, and steal the slaves; but, according to them, had we not been so impatient and flown to arms, the influence of Abe Lincoln and his fellow-abolitionists would not have affected the Southerners pecuniarily; for it might have been possible for Congress to compensate slave-owners, that is, by buying up all slaves, and afterwards setting them free.[24] But when the Southerners, who were not averse to selling slaves in the open market, refused to consider anything relating to them, and began to seize upon government property, forts, arsenals, and war-ships, and to set about establishing a separate system in the country, then the North resolved that this should not be, and that was the true reason of the war. The Northern people cared nothing for the "niggers,"—the slavery question could have been settled in another and quieter way,—but they cared all their lives were worth for their country.

At the river-side there was tremendous activity. There were seven or eight steamers tied to the bank, discharging troops and stores. The commissariat stores and forage lay in mountainous heaps. In one place on the slope was a corral of prisoners, about four hundred and fifty in number, who had been captured the day before. I was delivered to the charge of the officer in command of the guards, and, in a few minutes, was left to my own reflections amid the unfortunates.

The loss of the Union troops in the two days' fight was 1754 killed, 8408 wounded, and 2885 captured; total, 13,047. That of the Confederates was 1728 killed, 8012 wounded, and 959 missing; total, 10,699.[25]

The loss of Hindman's Brigade was 109 killed, 546 wounded, 38

---

24. Throughout the *Autobiography* HMS's feelings about slavery remain ambivalent. Thirty years later he would meet Booker T. Washington who was visiting the House of Commons. They would discuss Africa and its relation to the Black American. After their conversation, Washington would be "more convinced than ever that there was no hope of the American Negro improving his condition by emigrating to Africa" (Booker T. Washington, *Up From Slavery* [1901; reprint, Boston: Houghton Mifflin, 1928], 206).

25. HMS accepts figures provided by Grant in his *Century* article (Grant, "Battle of Shiloh," *B&L*, 1:485).

missing; total, 693,—about a fifth of the number that went, on the Sunday morning, into action.[26]

Referring to these totals, 1754 + 1728 = 3482, killed, General Grant, however, says, in his article on Shiloh: "This estimate of the Confederate loss must be incorrect. We buried, by actual count, more of the enemy's dead in front of the divisions of McClernand and Sherman alone than here reported; and 4000 was the estimate of the burial parties for the whole field."[27]

Nine days after the battle of Shiloh, a conscript law was passed by the Confederate Congress which annulled all previous contracts made with volunteers, and all men between eighteen and thirty-five were to be soldiers during the continuance of the war. General T. C. Hindman, our brigade commander, was appointed, fifty days after Shiloh, commanding general of Arkansas, and enforced the conscript law remorselessly. He collected an army of 20,000 under this law, and such as deserted were shot by scores, until he made himself odious to all by his ruthlessness, violence, and tyranny.[28]

While at Atlanta, Georgia, in March, 1891, I received the following letter (which is copied verbatim) from "old Slate," as we used to call him, owing to a certain quaint, old-mannish humour which characterised him.

Blue Ridge, Ga.
March 28th, 1891

Dear Sir,—I am anxious to know if you enlisted in Company E., Dixie Greys, 6th Arkansas Regiment, Col Lyon commanding, Lieut.-Col. Haw-

---

26. Hindman himself was wounded on Sunday, April 6, 1862, and never submitted a report of the battle (*OR*, 10[1]:568–69).

27. Numbers of losses for battles such as Shiloh are almost impossible to reconstruct precisely, for commanding generals or for historians. Nevertheless, in a recent assessment Daniel puts the losses (killed and wounded) of the respective armies at 13,047 (USA), 10,699 (CSA) (Grant, "Battle of Shiloh," *B&L*, 1:485; Daniel, *Shiloh*, 305, 322).

28. For his performance at Shiloh, Hindman was rewarded with promotion to major general and division command, and on May 26, 1862, the War Department ordered him to take charge of the newly formed "Trans-Mississippi District encompassing Arkansas, Missouri, Indian Territory, and the portion of Louisiana north of the Red River." Hindman faced an impossible task, but set to work with great energy. His actions, however, resulted in criticism from every quarter, and ultimately he was recalled east of the Mississippi January 30, 1863. It is not known why HMS felt so strongly about Hindman (*OR*, 52[2]:303; Neal and Kremm, *Lion of the South*, 113–14, 125–56).

thorn, Capt. Smith commanding Dixie Greys, Co. E. Col. Lyon was accidently killed on the Tennessee River, by riding off Bluff and horse falling on him.[29]

On the 6th April, 1862, the Confederates attacked the Yankees at Shiloh. Early in the morning I was wounded, and I never saw our boyish-looking Stanley no more, but understood he was captured, and sent North. I have read everything in newspapers, and your Histories, believing you are the same Great Boy. We all loved you, and regretted the results of that eventful day. This is enough for you to say, in reply, that you are the identical Boyish Soldier. You have wrote many letters for me. Please answer by return mail.

Very truly yours,
J. M. Slate

Address: J. M. Slate, Blue Ridge

29. It is surprising that HMS does not mention in the *Autobiography* the death of Regimental Commander Lyon (October 11, 1861).

7

Prisoner of War

On the 8th of April we were embarked on a steamer, and despatched to St. Louis.[1] We were a sad lot of men. I feel convinced that most of them felt, with myself, that we were ill-starred wretches, and special objects of an unkind Fate. We made no advances to acquaintanceship, for what was the value of any beggarly individual amongst us? All he possessed in the world was a thin, dingy suit of grey, and every man's thoughts were of his own misfortune, which was as much as he could bear, without being bothered with that of another.

On the third day, I think, we reached St. Louis, and were marched through the streets, in column of fours, to a Ladies' College, or some such building. On the way, we were not a little consoled to find that we had sympathisers, especially among the ladies, in the city.[2] They crowded the sidewalks, and smiled kindly, and sometimes cheered, and waved dainty white handkerchiefs at us. How beautiful and clean they appeared, as compared with our filthy selves! While at the college, they besieged the building, and threw fruit and cakes at the struggling crowds in the windows, and in many ways assisted to lighten the gloom on our spirits.[3]

1. The capture of HMS at Shiloh and his subsequent imprisonment at Camp Douglas and enlistment in Company L, First Illinois Light Artillery, are substantiated in Letters Received by the Enlisted Branch, File #3739-C (EB) 1885, RG 94: Records of the Adjutant General's Office, NA.

2. "In a diary, made up later from notes put together soon afterwards, he writes: 'April 13, 1862. Arrived in St. Louis, put in college. People St. Louis very generous. Ladies sent presents of food and flowers' " (Hall, *Stanley*, 130).

3. A preview of the reception received by HMS had come six weeks earlier to Fort Donelson prisoners who were being shipped to Camp Chase. The prisoners had remained on board the *Hiawatha* in sight of the St. Louis citizens, many of whom waved

Four days later, we were embarked on railroad cars, and taken across the State of Illinois to Camp Douglas,[4] on the outskirts of Chicago.[5] Our prison-pen was a square and spacious enclosure, like a bleak cattle-yard, walled high with planking, on the top of which, at every sixty yards or so, were sentry-boxes. About fifty feet from its base, and running parallel with it, was a line of lime-wash. That was the "deadline," and any prisoner who crossed it was liable to be shot.

One end of the enclosure contained the offices of the authorities. Colonel James A. Milligan [sic], one of the Irish Brigade (killed at Winchester, July 24th, 1864) commanded the camp.[6] Mr. Shipman, a citizen of Chicago, acted as chief commissary.[7] At the other end, at quite three hundred yards distance, were the buildings allotted to the prisoners, huge, barn-like structures of planking, each about two hundred and fifty

---

their handkerchiefs encouragingly and attempted to give them apples (Nathaniel F. Cheairs, *I'll Sting if I Can: The Life and Prison Letters of Major N. F. Cheairs, C.S.A.* ed. Nathaniel C. Hughes, Jr. [Signal Mountain, Tenn.: Mountain Press, 1998], 57. See also H. C. Lockhart to Catherine E. Lockhart, March 19, 1862, Harrison C. Lockhart Papers, Southern Historical Collection, University of North Carolina, Chapel Hill, N.C.).

4. During the spring of 1862 Confederate units "were broken up, the enlisted men being removed from the boat and put aboard trains for Camp Douglas, even farther north, up close to Chicago." Company grade officers were sent to Camp Chase, near Columbus, Ohio, while field grade officers went sent to Fort Warren, Massachusetts. Named for Stephen A. Douglas, the camp, which was built on his land, was first used for Federal trainees, then became a prison following the capture of Fort Donelson. By July 1862, soon after HMS left, the number of captives rose to 7,850 (Cheairs, *I'll Sting if I Can*, 57; Alexis A. Praus, *Confederate Soldiers, Sailors, and Civilians Who Died as Prisoners of War at Camp Douglas, Chicago, Ill., 1862–1865* [Kalamazoo, Mich.: Edgar Gray, n.d.], i–iii).

5. Stanley's official record as a Confederate soldier consists of a single card (undated) in his CSR containing the following information: H. Stanley, Company A, Sixth Regiment Arkansas, a prisoner at Camp Douglas, Illinois, who entered "The Irish Brigade." A further notation: "See also Bty. L, 1 Ill. Lt. Art. & U.S. Navy."

6. Col. James A. Mulligan, commander of the Twenty-third Illinois Volunteer Infantry (the "Irish brigade"), had commanded the force defending Lexington, Missouri, but was forced to surrender to Sterling Price, September 20, 1861. In March 1862, following his exchange the previous October, Mulligan took charge of Camp Douglas; all the while he was busy reorganizing the Twenty-third Illinois. He left the camp in June 1862. He would later command in western Virginia, meeting his death in the Battle of Winchester, July 26, 1864 (see James A. Mulligan, "The Siege of Lexington, Mo.," *B&L*, 1:307–13; Alfred T. Andreas, *History of Chicago* [1884; reprint, New York: Arno Press, 1975], 2:301).

7. HMS may have meant Harry M. Spaulding, a citizen of Rockford, Illinois, who had been appointed quartermaster in late summer 1861 (Andreas, *History of Chicago*, 2:301).

feet by forty, and capable of accommodating between two hundred and three hundred men. There may have been about twenty of these structures, about thirty feet apart, and standing in two rows; and I estimated that there were enough prisoners within it to have formed a strong brigade—say about three thousand men—when we arrived. I remember, by the regimental badges which they wore on their caps and hats, that they belonged to the three arms of the service, and that almost every Southern State was represented. They were clad in home-made butternut and grey.

To whatever it was due, the appearance of the prisoners startled me. The Southerners' uniforms were never pretty, but when rotten, and ragged, and swarming with vermin, they heightened the disreputability of their wearers; and, if anything was needed to increase our dejection after taking sweeping glances at the arid mud-soil of the great yard, the butternut and grey clothes, the sight of ash-coloured faces, and of the sickly and emaciated condition of our unhappy friends, were well calculated to do so.

We were led to one of the great wooden barns, where we found a six-foot wide platform on each side, raised about four feet above the flooring. These platforms formed continuous bunks for about sixty men, allowing thirty inches to each man. On the floor, two more rows of men could be accommodated. Several bales of hay were brought, out of which we helped ourselves for bedding. Blankets were also distributed, one to each man. I, fortunately, found a berth on the right-hand platform, not far from the doorway, and my mate was a young sprig of Mississippi nobility named W. H. Wilkes (a nephew of Admiral C. [Charles] Wilkes, U.S. Navy, the navigator, and captor of Mason and Slidell, Confederate Commissioners).

Mr. Shipman soon after visited us, and, after inspection, suggested that we should form ourselves into companies, and elect officers for drawing rations and superintending of quarters. I was elected captain of the right-hand platform and berths below it. Blank books were served out to each captain, and I took the names of my company, which numbered over a hundred. By showing my book at the commissariat, and bringing a detail with me, rations of soft bread, fresh beef, coffee, tea, potatoes, and salt, were handed to me by the gross, which I had afterwards to distribute to the chiefs of the messes.

On the next day (April 16th), after the morning duties had been performed, the rations divided, the cooks had departed contented, and the quarters swept, I proceeded to my nest and reclined alongside of my friend Wilkes, in a posture that gave me a command of one-half of the building. I made some remarks to him upon the card-playing groups opposite, when, suddenly, I felt a gentle stroke on the back of my neck, and, in an instant, I was unconscious. The next moment I had a vivid view of the village of Tremeirchion, and the grassy slopes of the hills of Hiraddog, and I seemed to be hovering over the rook woods of Bryn-bella. I glided to the bed-chamber of my Aunt Mary. My aunt was in bed, and seemed sick unto death. I took a position by the side of the bed, and saw myself, with head bent down, listening to her parting words, which sounded regretful, as though conscience smote her for not having been so kind as she might have been, or had wished to be. I heard the boy say, "I believe you, aunt. It is neither your fault, nor mine. You were good and kind to me, and I knew you wished to be kinder; but things were so ordered that you had to be what you were. I also dearly wished to love you, but I was afraid to speak of it, lest you would check me, or say something that would offend me. I feel our parting was in this spirit. There is no need of regrets. You have done your duty to me, and you had children of your own, who required all your care. What has happened to me since, was decreed should happen. Farewell."

I put forth my hand and felt the clasp of the long, thin hands of the sore-sick woman, I heard a murmur of farewell, and immediately I woke.

It appeared to me that I had but closed my eyes. I was still in the same reclining attitude, the groups opposite were still engaged in their card games, Wilkes was in the same position. Nothing had changed.

I asked, "What *has* happened?"

"What could happen?" said he. "What makes you ask? It is but a moment ago you were speaking to me."

"Oh, I thought I had been asleep a long time."

On the next day, the 17th April, 1862, my Aunt Mary died at Ffyn-non Beuno!

I believe that the soul of every human being has its attendant spirit—a nimble and delicate essence, whose method of action is by a subtle suggestion which it contrives to insinuate into the mind, whether asleep or awake. We are too gross to be capable understanding the signification of the dream, the vision, or the sudden presage, or of divining the source of the premonition, or its purport. We admit that we are liable to receive a fleeting picture of an act, or a figure, at any moment; but, except being struck by certain strange coincidences which happen to most of us, we seldom make an effort to unravel the mystery. The swift, darting messenger stamps an image on the mind, and displays a vision to the sleeper; and if, as sometimes follows, among tricks and twists of an errant mind, or reflex acts of the memory, it happens to be a true representation of what is to happen, or has happened, thousands of miles away, we are left to grope hopelessly as to the manner and meaning of it, for there is nothing tangible to lay hold of.

There are many things relating to my existence which are inexplicable to me, and probably it is best so; this death-bed scene, projected on my mind's screen, across four thousand five hundred miles of space, is one of these mysteries.

After Wilkes and I had thoroughly acquainted ourselves with all the evil and the good to be found at Camp Douglas, neither of us saw any reason at first why we could not wait with patience for the exchange of prisoners. But, as time passed, we found it to be a dreary task to endure the unchanging variety of misery surrounding us. I was often tempted with an impulse to challenge a malignant sentry's bullet, by crossing that ghastly "dead-line," which I saw every day I came out. A more unlovely sight than a sick Secessionist, in a bilious butternut, it is scarcely possible to conceive. Though he had been naked and soiled by his own filth, there would still have remained some elements of attractiveness in him; but that dirty, ill-made, nut-coloured homespun aggravated every sense, and made the poor, sickly wretch unutterably ugly.

In our treatment, I think there was a purpose. If so, it may have been from a belief that we should the sooner recover our senses by experiencing as much misery, pain, privation, and sorrow as could be contained within a prison; and, therefore, the authorities rigidly excluded every medical, pious, musical, or literary charity that might have alleviated our sufferings. It was a barbarous age, it is true; but there were sufficient Christian families in Chicago, who, I am convinced, only needed a suggestion, to have formed societies for the relief of the prisoners. And what an opportunity there was for such, to strengthen piety, to promote cheerfulness, soothe political ferocity, and subdue the brutal and vicious passions which possessed those thousands of unhappy youths immured within the horrible pen![8]

Left to ourselves, with absolutely nothing to do but to brood over our positions, bewail our lots, catch the taint of disease from each other, and passively abide our prison-pen, we were soon in a fair state of rotting, while yet alive. The reaction from the excitement of the battlefield, and the cheerful presence of exulting thousands, was suspended for a few days by travel up the Mississippi, the generosity of lady-sympathisers in St. Louis, and the trip across Illinois; but, after a few days, it set in strong upon us, when once within the bleak camp at Chicago. Everything we saw and touched added its pernicious influence—the melancholy faces of those who were already wearied with their confinement, the numbers of the sick, the premature agedness of the emaciated, the distressing degeneration of manhood, the plaints of suffering wretches, the increasing bodily discomfort from ever-multiplying vermin, which infested every square inch.

Within a week, our new draft commenced to succumb under the maleficent influences of our surroundings.[9] Our buildings swarmed with vermin, the dust-sweepings were alive with them. The men began to suffer from bilious disorders; dysentery and typhus began to rage. Day after day my company steadily diminished; and every morning I had to see them carried in their blankets to the hospital, whence none ever returned. Those not yet delirious, or too weak to move unaided, we kept with us; but the dysentery—however they contracted it—was of a peculiarly epidemical character, and its victims were perpetually passing us, trembling with weakness, or writhing with pain, exasperating our senses to such a degree that only the strong-minded could forego some expression of their disgust.

8. The descriptions of HMS are echoed in R. T. Bean, "Seventeen Months in Camp Douglas," *CV*, 22:268–70, 310–12. See also Joseph Eisendrath, Jr., "Chicago's Camp Douglas, 1861–1865," *Journal of the Illinois Historical Society* 53 (spring 1960):37–63; and George Levy's recent comprehensive study, *To Die in Chicago: Confederate Prisoners in Camp Douglas, 1862–65* (Gretna, La.: Pelican Publishing, 1999).

9. Camp Douglas had been established in the summer of 1861 as a camp of rendezvous and instruction for recruits from the Northern Military District of Illinois. Sickness among the recruits was widespread, however, and it was decided to abandon the unhealthy camp. Unfortunately for HMS and his fellow Confederates, Camp Douglas became a "United States military camp" or prison following the battle of Fort Donelson, February 1862 (Andreas, *History of Chicago*, 2:301).

The latrines were all at the rear of our plank barracks, and each time imperious nature compelled us to resort to them, we lost a little of that respect and consideration we owed our fellow-creatures. For, on the way thither, we saw crowds of sick men, who had fallen, prostrate from weakness, and given themselves wholly to despair; and, while they crawled or wallowed in their filth, they cursed and blasphemed as often as they groaned. In the edge of the gaping ditches, which provoked the gorge to look at, there were many of the sick people, who, unable to leave, rested there for hours, and made their condition hopeless by breathing the stenchful atmosphere. Exhumed corpses could not have presented anything more hideous than dozens of these dead-and-alive men, who, oblivious to the weather, hung over the latrines, or lay extended along the open sewer, with only a few gasps intervening between them and death. Such as were not too far gone prayed for death, saying, "Good God, let me die! Let me go, O Lord!" and one insanely damned his vitals and his constitution, because his agonies were so protracted. No self-respecting being could return from their vicinity without feeling bewildered by the infinite suffering, his existence degraded, and religion and sentiment blasted.

Yet, indoors, what did we see? Over two hundred unwashed, unkempt, uncombed men, in the dismalest attitudes, occupied in relieving themselves from hosts of vermin, or sunk in gloomy introspection, staring blankly, with heads between their knees, at nothing; weighed down by a surfeit of misery, internal pains furrowing their faces, breathing in a fine cloud of human scurf, and dust of offensive hay, dead to everything but the flitting fancies of the hopeless!

One intelligent and humane supervisor would have wrought wonders at this period with us, and arrested that swift demoralization with which we were threatened. None of us were conspicuously wise out of our own sphere; and of sanitary laws we were all probably as ignorant as of the etiology of sclerosis of the nerve-centres. In our colossal ignorance, we were perhaps doing something half-a-dozen times a day, as dangerous as eating poison, and constantly swallowing a few of the bacilli of typhus. Even had we possessed the necessary science at our finger-tips, we could not have done much, unaided by the authorities; but when the authorities were as ignorant as ourselves,—I cannot believe their neglect of us intentional,—we were simply doomed!

Every morning, the wagons came to the hospital and dead-house, to take away the bodies; and I saw the corpses rolled in their blankets, taken to the vehicles, and piled one upon another, as the New Zealand frozen-mutton carcases are carted from the docks!

The statistics of Andersonville are believed to show that the South was even more callous towards their prisoners than the authorities of Camp Douglas were. I admit that we were better fed than the Union prisoners were, and against Colonel Milligan and Mr. Shipman I have not a single accusation to make. It was the age that was brutally sense-less, and heedlessly cruel. It was lavish and wasteful of life, and had not the least idea of what civilised warfare ought to be, except in strategy. It was at the end of the flint-lock age, a stupid and heartless age, which believed that the application of every variety of torture was better for discipline than kindness, and was guilty, during the war, of enormities that would tax the most saintly to forgive.

Just as the thirties were stupider and crueller than the fifties, and the fifties were more bloody than the seventies, in the mercantile marine service, so a war in the nineties will be much more civilized than the Civil War of the sixties. Those who have survived that war, and have seen brotherly love re-established, and reconciliation completed, when they think of Andersonville, Libby, Camp Douglas, and other prisons, and of the blood shed in 2261 battles and skirmishes, must in this pres-ent peaceful year needs think that a moral epidemic raged, to have made them so intensely hate then what they profess to love now. Though a democratic government like the American will always be more despotic and arbitrary than that of a constitutional monarchy, even its army will have its Red Cross societies, and Prisoners' Aid Society; and the sights we saw at Camp Douglas will never be seen in America again.[10]

Were Colonel Milligan living now, he would admit that a better sys-tem of latrines, a ration of soap, some travelling arrangements for lava-tories, a commissioned superintendent over each barrack, a brass band,

10. Levy discredits HMS's "famous chronicle of suffering," considering it at best "fanciful." Indeed, Levy feels strongly that HMS was never a prisoner at Camp Douglas: "His story is a hoax." For that matter, HMS may never have been a private in the Sixth Arkansas. Levy bases his contention on the muster rolls of the Sixth Arkansas; the lack of a CSR for HMS; Confederate Prisoners of War, 1861–65, Roll 56; and the Report of the Illinois Adjutant General, vol. 8. "In addition," Levy continues, "there was no Henry Stanley, or H. Stanley, in Battery L, 1st Illinois Light Artillery, which he supposedly joined" (Levy, *To Die in Chicago*, 70–72, 380n).

the loan of a few secondhand books, magazines, and the best-class newspapers (with all war-news cut out), would have been the salvation of two-thirds of those who died at Camp Douglas; and, by showing how superior the United States Government was to the Confederate States, would have sent the exchanged prisoners back to their homes in a spirit more reconciled than they were.[11] Those in authority today also know that, though when in battle it is necessary to fight with all the venom of fiends for victory, once the rifle is laid down, and a man becomes a prisoner, a gracious treatment is more efficacious than the most revolting cruelty. Still, the civilized world is densely ignorant. It has improved immensely in thirty years, but from what I have seen in my travels in many lands, it is less disposed to be kind to man than to any other creatures; and yet, none of all God's creatures is more sadly in need of protection than he!

The only official connected with Camp Douglas whom I remember with pleasure is Mr. Shipman, the commissary. He was gentlemanly and white-haired, which, added to his unvarying benevolence and politeness, caused him to be regarded by me as something of an agreeable wonder in that pestful yard. After some two days' acquaintance, while drawing the rations, he sounded me as to my intentions. I scarcely comprehended him at the outset, for Camp Douglas was not a place to foster intentions. He explained that, if I were tired of being a prisoner, I could be released by enrolling myself as a Unionist, that is, becoming a Union soldier. My eyes opened very wide at this, and I shook my head, and said, "Oh, no, I could not do that." Nothing could have been more unlikely; I had not even dreamed that such an act was possible.

A few days later, I said to Mr. Shipman, "They have taken two wagon-loads of dead men away this morning." He gave a sympathetic shrug, as if to say, "It was all very sad, but what can we do?" He then held forth upon the superiority of the North, the certainty of defeat for the South, the pity it was to see young men throw their lives away for such a cause as slavery, and so on; in short, all that a genuinely kind man, but fervidly Northern, could say. His love embraced Northerners and Southerners alike, for he saw no distinction between them, except

11. Levy would disagree. Mulligan "was anxious to get back to the war," Levy believes, and "did not care to make a permanent contribution to the camp." Mulligan "made his own rules to keep the prisoners in line" (ibid., 105–106).

that the younger brother had risen to smite the elder, and must be punished until he repented.

But it was useless to try and influence me by political reasons. In the first place, I was too ignorant in politics, and too slow of comprehension, to follow his reasonings; in the second place, every American friend of mine was a Southerner, and my adopted father was a Southerner, and I was blind through my gratitude; and, in the third place, I had a secret scorn for people who could kill one another for the sake of African slaves. There were no blackies in Wales, and why a sooty-faced nigger from a distant land should be an element of disturbance between white brothers, was a puzzle to me. I should have to read a great deal about him, ascertain his wrongs and his rights, and wherein his enslavement was unjust and his liberty was desirable, before I could venture upon giving an opinion adverse to 20,000,000 Southerners. As I had seen him in the South, he was a half-savage, who had been exported by his own countrymen, and sold in the open market, agreeable to time-honoured custom. Had the Southerners invaded Africa and made captives of the blacks, I might have seen some justice in decent and pious people exclaiming against the barbarity. But, so far as I knew of the matter, it was only the accident of a presidential election which had involved the North and South in a civil war, and I could not take it upon me to do anything more than stand by my friends.

But, in the course of six weeks, more powerful influences than Mr. Shipman's gentle reasoning were undermining my resolve to remain as a prisoner. These were the increase in sickness, the horrors of the prison, the oily atmosphere, the ignominious cartage of the dead, the useless flight of time, the fear of being incarcerated for years, which so affected my spirits that I felt a few more days of these scenes would drive me mad. Finally, I was persuaded to accept with several other prisoners the terms of release,[12] and enrolled myself in the U.S. Artillery

12. Levy believes such a release would have come about because "Colonel Mulligan, without authority, was releasing Englishmen by order of the British Consul in Chicago." Clayton D. Laurie, on the other hand, contends that Mulligan "discovered many Confederates captured at Forts Henry and Donelson were Irish-born and willing to fight for the Union in return for their release. He inquired of Union Major General Henry Halleck about the possibility of raising Federal units from among foreign-born Confederate prisoners and received a vague but positive response" (Levy, *To Die in Chicago*, 71; Clayton D. Laurie, "Two-Sided Adventure," *Civil War Times Illustrated* 24 [June 1985]: 44–45).

Service,[13] and, on the 4th June was once more free to inhale the fresh air.[14]

But, after two or three days' service, the germs of the prison-disease, which had swept so many scores of fine young fellows to untimely graves, broke out with virulence in my system. I disguised my complaint as much as was possible, for, having been a prisoner, I felt myself liable to be suspected; but, on the day of our arrival at Harper's Ferry, dysentery and low fever laid me prostrate.[15] I was conveyed to the hospital, and remained there until the 22nd June, when I was discharged out of the service, a wreck.

My condition at this time was as low as it would be possible to reduce a human being to, outside of an American prison. I had not a penny in my pocket; a pair of blue military trousers clothed my nethers, a dark serge coat covered my back, and a mongrel hat my head. I knew not where to go: the seeds of disease were still in me, and I could not walk three hundred yards without stopping to gasp for breath. As, like a log, I lay at night under the stars, heated by fever, and bleeding internally, I thought I ought to die, according to what I had seen of those who yielded to death. As my strength departed, death advanced; and there was no power or wish to resist left in me. But with each dawn there would come a tiny bit of hope, which made me forget all about death, and think only of food, and of the necessity of finding a shelter. Hagerstown is but twenty-four miles from Harper's Ferry; but it took me a week to reach a farm-house not quite half-way. I begged permission to occupy an out-house, which may have been used to store corn, and the farmer consented. My lips were scaled with the fever, eyes swimming,

---

13. HMS enlisted for three years in Battery L, First Illinois Light Artillery, at Chicago, June 7, 1862. He gave his age as twenty-two, five feet six inches in height, blue eyes, auburn hair, born in New York City, occupation: laborer. When Battery L moved east to New Creek, West Virginia, that summer, HMS went with them (*OR Supp.*, part 2, 8:306, 368).

14. HMS, in a long letter to Katie Gough-Roberts in 1869, told the story of his life including his imprisonment at Camp Douglas. In this version, however, he escaped by "dodging the bullets of a dozen sentries" and "plunging into a river and swimming to liberty" (McLynn, *Stanley*, 42–43. See also Jones and Wynne, *Stanley and Wales*, 22).

15. Battery L remained at New Creek, West Virginia, for over a year, then moved on to Petersburg, West Virginia. On August 18, 1862, HMS is shown as having been hospitalized at Harper's Ferry June 22, 1862, "and not heard from." He would be carried as "absent" until July 31, 1863, when he would be declared a deserter (HMS CSR, RG 94, NA).

face flushed red, under the layer of a week's dirt—the wretchedest object alive, possibly, as I felt I was, by the manner the good fellow tried to hide his disgust. What of it? He spread some hay in the out-house, and I dropped on it without the smallest wish to leave again. It was several days before I woke to consciousness, to find a mattress under me, and different clothes on me. I had a clean cotton shirt, and my face and hands were without a stain. A man named Humphreys was attending to me, and he was the deputy of the farmer in his absence. By dint of assiduous kindness, and a diet of milk, I gained strength slowly, until I was able to sit in the orchard, when, with open air, exercise, and more generous food, I rapidly mended. In the early part of July, I was able to assist in the last part of the harvest, and to join in the harvest supper.

The farm-house where my Good Samaritan lived is situated close to the Hagerstown pike—a few miles beyond Sharpsburg. My friend's name is one of the few that has escaped my memory. I stayed with him until the middle of August, well-fed and cared for, and when I left him he insisted on driving to me Hagerstown, and paying my railway fare to Baltimore, via Harrisburg.[16]

16. DTS added the following note at this point: "Stanley remembered, afterwards, that the farm-house belonged to a Mr. Baker, and that, in June, 1862, he had walked there from Harper's Ferry—three miles from Sharpsburg, and nine miles from Hagerstown. Mr. Baker's house seemed to have been near the cross-roads—near the extreme left flank of McClellan's army" (Stanley, *Autobiography*, 215n).

Epilogue

Stanley's *Autobiography* ends abruptly in August 1862 as he prepared to set out for Baltimore. According to his United States Army compiled service record, he had not been discharged from the hospital at Harper's Ferry. Quite the contrary. He simply had left, walked off, deserted.[1] Now a fugitive, he made his way to Baltimore where he sought out the fiancée of his prison friend W. H. Wilkes. Whether he received

---

1. HMS's experience in the United States Army would haunt him. Twenty years later, after he had become an international celebrity, HMS wrote Secretary of War William C. Endicott requesting that the charge of desertion be removed from his record and that he be issued an honorable discharge:

> I, Henry M. Stanley, do solemnly declare and affirm as follows, to wit: when I enlisted at Chicago I was a boy 18 years of age, my condition physically very much reduced by prison life, I then served with my company, doing honorable duty until I was prostrated by a wasting disease from which I suffered for two months, after which I was discharged from the hospital having received a certificate the contents of which I at this day forget, but I well remember that I was so feeble as to be incapable of service. I understood and believed that the certificate was an honorable discharge and acted upon that understanding and belief. My weight at the time I left the hospital was about 95 lbs. and I did not recover my health and strength until six months had elapsed. After my enlistment and to this day, I was and have been loyal to the Union and the American flag. To the best of my recollection I entered the hospital in the early months of 1863, and was discharged about March or April, 1863. Owing to the disease from which I suffered my memory of those events is exceedingly imperfect.

Endicott took a personal interest in HMS's request and ordered the adjutant general, Brig. Gen. R. C. Drum, to make a close investigation. Although no new evidence surfaced, the adjutant general's office decided, because of Stanley's affidavit and "the loss of

help from the young lady is unknown, but he did remain in the Baltimore vicinity for a number of weeks, working as a hand on an oyster-schooner. When he had accumulated sufficient funds for his passage, he embarked on the *E. Sherman*, bound for Liverpool.[2]

Upon his arrival in England in the winter of 1862 to 1863, Stanley set out immediately for Denbigh to see his mother, Elizabeth Parry. He found that she had married in 1860 and that she and her husband, Robert Jones, were proprietors of a small inn. The meeting at their home was brief and devastating. "I was told that 'I was a disgrace to them in the eyes of their neighbours,'" reported Stanley, "'and they desired me to leave as speedily as possible.'"[3]

According to Lady Stanley, the disheartened young man then returned to America. Evidence, however, for Stanley's activities from November 1862 to June 1864 is quite sketchy. He shipped back to New York City as a hand on the *Ernestine* and then signed on various merchant vessels "for voyages between Boston and Mediterranean ports." Dorothy Stanley found a diary fragment among his papers showing that he was shipwrecked at Barcelona, but, according to biographers Hall, Bierman, McLynn, and Thomas George, he was not shipwrecked at all, but jumped ship, being detained temporarily by Spanish authorities when he swam ashore. Somewhat later he was arrested by French officials before making his way back to the United States.

For about six months Stanley was a clerk for Notary Public Thomas Erwin Hughes in Brooklyn before enlisting in the Union Navy for three years, "giving his age (falsely) as twenty and apparently concealing the fact that he had considerable experience as a merchant seaman, for he was marked down by the naval recruiting officer as a 'landsman.'" Apparently he also concealed the fact that he was a deserter from the First Illinois Light Artillery.[4]

Stanley joined the crew of the *USS North Carolina*, a receiving ship,

---

many records appertaining to the post at Harper's Ferry," to remove the charge of desertion and to issue HMS an honorable discharge, May 15, 1885 (Letters Received by the Enlisted Branch, File #3739-C [EB] 1885, RG 94, NA).

2. Stanley, *Autobiography*, 219.

3. Ibid., 219. See also Jones and Wynne, *H. M. Stanley and Wales*, 17; Hall, *Stanley*, 132.

4. Bierman, *Dark Safari*, 36–37. See also Hall, *Stanley*, 133–35; McLynn, *Stanley*, 44–45; Thomas George, *The Birth, Boyhood, and Younger Days of Henry Stanley* (London: Roxburghen Press, 1895), 103.

then soon was transferred to the warship *USS Minnesota*.[5] It was on the latter ship, in the capacity of ship's writer or clerk, that Stanley witnessed the bungled attack on Fort Fisher, North Carolina, December 7–27, 1864, by an amphibious force under Major General Benjamin F. Butler.[6] Infuriated by Butler's ineptness and failure to carry out orders, Commander-in-Chief General Ulysses S. Grant relieved Butler of command and sent him home to Massachusetts to sit out the remainder of the war.[7] Energetic and capable Brigadier General Alfred H. Terry replaced Butler and in mid-January 1865 led a well-coordinated assault that resulted in the capture of this "Gibraltar of the Confederacy." The *Minnesota* played a prominent role in both operations. Stanley, ship's writer, observed.[8]

Following the fall of Fort Fisher, Stanley sailed north on the *Minne-*

5. According to Lady Stanley, HMS served as writer aboard the *USS Moses H. Stuyvesant* during the Fort Fisher expeditions. This seems unlikely. The few naval records extant that mention HMS's service do not mention the ship; furthermore the *Stuyvesant* does not seem to have played a role in the attacks at all (see U.S. Navy Department, *Official Records of the Union and Confederate Navies in the War of the Rebellion*, vols. 11 and 27 [Washington, D.C.: U.S. Government Printing Office, 1894–1927]. See also Ella Lonn, *Foreigners in the Confederacy* [Chapel Hill: University of North Carolina Press, 1940], 198–99, 307).

6. "By an odd coincidence, a fortnight before Stanley arrived off Fort Fisher, another young Briton with whose surname his own would forever be linked died inland in North Carolina, a prisoner of the Confederates. Like Stanley, this young private had assumed a new name in America, calling himself Rupert Vincent. Shortly before he died he wrote home to his father: '. . . I am convinced that to bear your name here would lead to further dishonours to it.' His father, Dr. David Livingstone, was at that moment preparing for his last great expedition to the interior of Africa" (Hall, *Stanley*, 136. See also Stanley, *Autobiography*, 220).

7. Stanley, *Autobiography*, 220.

8. HMS claimed to have been transferred to the *USS Ticonderoga* just before the assault and played a hero's role. McLynn determined that "Stanley was neither on the *Ticonderoga* nor in any way involved in this second battle. This did not prevent him from concocting his most elaborate fantasy yet, in which he becomes the hero of the entire engagement. In Stanley's version, he swam 500 yards under fire and tied a rope to a Confederate ship, so that the *Ticonderoga* was able to secure her as a prize" (McLynn, *Stanley*, 47, 337n).

Navy Department records offer scant assistance since the Navy "did not begin to maintain personnel files for enlisted men until 1885." Ship muster rolls, however, confirm HMS enlisted July 19, 1864, at New York for a term of three years, listing his place of birth as Ireland, his occupation "landsman." His rating was "ship's writer." He served aboard the *USS Minnesota* and the *USS North Carolina*. No place nor date of discharge is given (K. Carter, National Archives 1 Reference Branch, Textual Reference Division, to

sota. When they docked at Portsmouth, New Hampshire, on February 10, 1865, he and a young shipmate, Lewis Noe, deserted using a pass forged by Stanley. They simply strolled past the guards, out the gates of the shipyard, and headed for New York City.[9] There they parted company, Noe joining a New York infantry regiment, while Stanley went from newspaper office to newspaper office vainly trying to sell pieces he had written about the Fort Fisher attacks. Then, ever impatient and restless, Stanley was off to St. Louis where the editor of the *Missouri Democrat* agreed to employ him on a freelance basis. To find his topics, his stories, Stanley continued west, through Salt Lake City and over the Sierras via the Donner Pass. He stayed in California only a short time, however, soon doubling back to Colorado where he remained until the spring of 1866.[10]

Adventure followed adventure out West as Stanley prospected for gold, shoveled quartz into a crusher, constructed a flatboat and journeyed down the Platte River, and tried his hand at printing. Later in 1866 an impetuous trip to China by way of Turkey ended in capture, torture, and imprisonment after which Stanley, in an attempt to trans-

---

Nathaniel C. Hughes, Jr., December 22, 1998. See also the *New York Sun*, August 24, 1872).

9. Lewis Noe wrote the editor of the *Sun*: "Early in February, 1865, . . . Stanley forged a pass, affixing the Commodore's name to it, permitting Stanley and myself to pass the gate of the navy yard. Once without the gate, we took off our sailor clothing, under which we wore suits of citizens' clothes, that had been procured through the aid of carpenters who were at work in the navy yard. We were now free to go where we pleased" (*New York Sun*, August 24, 1872. See also Bierman, *Dark Safari*, 38–39; Hall, *Stanley*, 139).

10. DTS writes of this time: "Then, for a twelve-month, his diary gives only such glimpses of him as an occasional name of a place with date. 'St. Joseph, Missouri,—across the Plains,—Indians,—Salt Lake City,—Denver,—Black Hawk,—Omaha.' Apparently through this time, he was impelled by an overflowing youthful energy, and an innate love of novelty and adventure.

"In his later years, he told how, in his early days, his exuberant vigour was such, that when a horse stood across his path his impulse was, not to go round, but to jump over it! And he had a keen relish for the sights and novelties, the many-coloured life of the West. So he went light-heartedly on his way,

'For to admire and for to see,
For to behold the world so wide.'

"Through this period he seems to have done more or less newspaper correspondence, and to have tended towards that as a profession. Here belongs an episode which is told in one of the autobiographic fragments; the reckless frolic of boys recounted with the sobriety of age" (Stanley, *Autobiography*, 221).

form ashes into hot coals, made his way back to Denbigh, his old home in Wales, to impress his mother and childhood friends with an officer's uniform he had made—passing himself off as an ensign in the United States Navy on leave from his warship the *USS Ticonderoga* on station in Constantinople. This time, apparently, his family received him warmly.

In 1867 Stanley returned to the American West lecturing about his hair-raising adventures in Turkey and covering as a correspondent a campaign launched by General Winfield Scott Hancock against the Cheyenne in Kansas and Nebraska. Thus Private Stanley would ride side-by-side with Generals Sherman and Custer and Sheridan, not to speak of Wild Bill Hickock, all the while raining colorful dispatches back, not only on editors' desks in St. Louis, but in Chicago and Cincinnati.[11] Soon his pieces were in demand nationally, and boldly he set off east to exploit his success, offering himself to James Gordon Bennett, Jr., and the *New York Herald*. He would cover, as special correspondent, the British expedition against Abyssinia. Bennett, impressed by the appeal of Stanley's western stories and the man's audacity, took him on. By a clever bribe to the head telegraphist in Suez, Egypt, the Yankee journalist Stanley was able to "scoop the field" in Abyssinia, and his stories hit the presses before his British competitors' did. The accounts he sent back created a public sensation, not to speak of "something very like a howl of indignation" from an angry British press.[12] His international reputation as an outstanding war correspondent nevertheless was established. "A life of railway celerity" followed his return from Abyssinia—Cairo, Paris, London, Athens, Aden, a Greek rebellion on Crete, a civil war in Spain.

Then an urgent telegram from Bennett summoned Stanley from Madrid to Paris, and on October 17, 1869, they met in Bennett's bedroom.[13] Bennett asked Stanley if he had any ideas about where to find the missionary Dr. David Livingstone, who had virtually disappeared

---

11. HMS collected his 1867 letters from the Indian country and published them in the first volume of *My Early Travels and Adventures in America and Asia* (1895). He believed the lessons learned in dealing with the American Indian were "very applicable to Africa." The second volume covers his 1868 Abyssinian expedition and missions to Egypt, India, and Spain.

12. McLynn, *Stanley*, 69; see also Hall, *Stanley*, 159–64.

13. Hall, *Stanley*, 172.

three years earlier in search of the heart of central Africa. Stanley replied he knew nothing of the explorer's whereabouts.

"I really do not know, sir!" Stanley repeated.

"Do you think he is alive?" asked Bennett.

"He may be and he may not be," Stanley answered.[14]

Thereupon Bennett told his celebrated correspondent that he wanted him to find Livingstone and interview him. Stanley reminded Bennett of the costs, of the enormity of such an enterprise, but Bennett was adamant. Draw what you need and continue to draw whatever it will take, the publisher replied, "BUT FIND LIVINGSTONE!"[15]

The story of this expedition is very well known, Stanley's meeting with David Livingstone being one of the dramatic high moments not only of Stanley's life but, indeed, of the nineteenth century. Stanley was at his best in Africa—on this expedition—determined, resourceful, valiant. He wired Bennett from Tabora in typical Stanley fashion:

> Until I hear more of him [Livingstone] or see the long absent old man face to face I bid you a farewell; but wherever he is be sure I shall not give up the chase. If alive you shall hear what he has to say; if dead I will find and bring his bones to you.[16]

The journey to Ujiji, "the trading center on Lake Tanganyika where Livingstone was believed to be," proved difficult, but Stanley persisted, overcoming illness, desertion by porters, a local war, treacherous terrain, and a thousand dangers. Finally he found the elderly missionary, who, by 1871, had become "almost a synonym for self-sacrificing idealism," in desperate health and despondent.[17] Stanley, acting against his own self-interest, remained with Livingstone for four months and became deeply attached to the missionary-explorer. It has been suggested by at least one biographer that Stanley had found the father figure he had sought so long. Perhaps. At the outset, certainly, David Livingstone was just another story, another assignment, but presently the ever-calculating Stanley found himself captive to the good doctor's earnestness and determination. Stanley found himself pleading with Living-

---

14. Bierman, *Dark Safari*, 74–75, quoting Stanley's journal, Stanley Family Archives.

15. Hall, *Stanley*, 172; McLynn, *Stanley*, 80.

16. Hall, *Stanley*, 187.

17. Hall, *Stanley*, 182; 193–94.

Dr. David Livingstone

stone to return to England with him, but the old man stood firm against all of Stanley's arguments and refused to abandon his exploration for the source of the Nile.[18]

On March 14, 1872, Stanley and Livingstone parted, their names forever linked. Stanley made his way back to Paris, then to London, finding himself instantly immortalized. He had little time, however, to enjoy the "whirl of cabs, soirées, dinners, dress-clothes and gloves," for he had determined he must defend himself against charges that the whole adventure was a fraud.[19] Writing furiously, Stanley completed *How I Found Livingstone* and published it on the eve of his departure for New York in November 1872. The work was "more than 700 pages long, with six maps and fifty-three illustrations by himself. It sold by tens of thousands and was into its third edition by Christmas."[20] Stanley

18. For clear, detailed accounts of Stanley's expedition and relationship with Livingstone, see Hall, *Stanley*, 176–207; Bierman, *Dark Safari*, 90–123; and McLynn, *Stanley*, 90–187.

19. Hall, *Stanley*, 214–15.

20. McLynn, *Stanley*, 224.

Lady Dorothy Tennant Stanley

excelled at self-promotion, of course, but it has been conceded that he was "the most assiduous foreign correspondent who ever lived."[21]

More assignments and commemorative metals and publications followed, but Stanley had made up his mind to complete the explorations begun by Dr. Livingstone, who had died in 1873. Stanley, according to African historian Alan Moorehead, was "a man of iron, an adventurer who was every bit as hard and ruthless as the world in which he lived."[22] Financed by the *New York Herald*, Stanley set out the following year from Zanzibar headed for Lake Victoria. The journey lasted three years and resulted in important discoveries and brought important changes in central Africa. Another book followed—*Through the Dark Continent* (1878). From 1879 to 1884 Stanley continued his work in the Congo, laying the foundation for what would become the Belgian Congo Free State. The harsh methods he employed with the natives, however, have blighted Stanley's name to this day.

21. Alan Moorehead, *The White Nile* (New York: Harper & Brothers, 1960), 111–12.
22. Ibid., 112.

Henry Morton Stanley in 1885 at age forty-four

Stanley's last expedition (1886–1890) would be to rescue the governor of the Equatorial Province of Egypt, Emin Pasha. Again Stanley was successful, overcoming enormous obstacles and opening up great unexplored areas including the Ruwenzori Range and the Semliki River linking Lakes Edward and Albert. This adventure would be related by Stanley in the book *In Darkest Africa* (1890).

That same year Stanley married Dorothy "Dolly" Tennant, and he and his bride went to the United States on a lecture tour. Upon arriving in New Orleans, Dolly Stanley reported that Stanley "tried to find the houses and places he had known as a boy." Unfortunately, he succeeded only in antagonizing the citizenry by refusing to call upon the sister of his foster mother, Mrs. Henry Hope Stanley, and avoiding (and refusing to receive) his old boyhood friends.[23]

Stanley's remaining years would be spent in England, although he

23. Kendall, "Old New Orleans Houses," 815; Stanley, *Autobiography*, 93n; Bierman, *Dark Safari*, 29; Hall, *Stanley*, 120.

made a long visit to South Africa in 1897, which he publicized in *Through South Africa* (1898). Honors continued to be heaped upon him, and in 1899 he was knighted by Queen Victoria. In the meantime, "lest I fly away again to Africa," he had entered politics and was elected to Parliament in 1895 by the citizens of North Lambert. He served until 1900.[24]

In 1899, in an engaging example of human symmetry, the betrayed and forsaken Stanley and his wife, Dolly, adopted a son, Denzil, from relatives in Denbighshire. Five years later, on May 10, 1904, Stanley died after a long illness. His dream of being buried in Westminster Abbey beside David Livingstone was denied. No reason was given.[25]

24. Hall, *Stanley*, 345.
25. Hall, *Stanley*, 351, 353.

SELECTED BIBLIOGRAPHY

PRIMARY SOURCES
Manuscript Collections

DeWitt, Arkansas
  Arkansas County Courthouse
    Marriage Book 1
Fort Smith, Arkansas
  Fort Smith Public Library
    W. J. and J. F. Weaver, "Early Days in Fort Smith"
London, England
  British Library
    Stanley Family Archives (originals at Musee Royal de l'Afrique Centrale,
      Tervuren, copies in British Library)
Washington, D.C.
  National Archives
    RG 109, War Department Collection of Confederate Records
      H. Stanley Compiled Service Record
      Complied Service Records of Confederate Generals and Staff Officers
        and Nonregimental Enlisted Men
    RG 94, Records of the Adjutant General's Office
      H. M. Stanley Compiled Service Record
      Letters Received by the Enlisted Branch

Collected Works, Letters, Diaries, Memoirs, and Reminiscences

Bennett, Norman R., ed. *Stanley's Dispatches to the New York Herald, 1871–1872, 1874–1877.* Boston: Boston University Press, 1970.

Buell, Don Carlos. "Shiloh Reviewed." *Battles and Leaders*. 1:487–539.

Gardner, Charles. *Gardner's New Orleans Directory for the Year 1859*. New Orleans: C. Gardner, 1858.

Grant, Ulysses S. "The Battle of Shiloh." *Battles and Leaders*. 1:465–86.

Johnson, Robert Underwood, and Clarence Clough Buel, eds. *Battles and Leaders of the Civil War, Being for the Most Part Contributions by Union and Confederate Officers: Based Upon "The Century" War Series*. 4 vols. New York: Century, 1887–1888.

Liddell, St. John R. *Liddell's Record*. Edited by Nathaniel C. Hughes, Jr. 1985. Reprint, Baton Rouge: Louisiana State University Press, 1997.

Mulligan, James A. "The Siege of Lexington, Mo." *Battles and Leaders*. 1:307–13.

Stanley, Henry Morton. *The Autobiography of Sir Henry Morton Stanley*. Edited by Dorothy T. Stanley. New York: Houghton Mifflin, 1909.

———. *My Early Travels and Adventures in America and Asia*. 2 vols. London: S. Low, Marston, 1895.

Yeary, Mamie. *Reminiscences of the Boys in Gray, 1861–1865*. Dallas, Texas: Smith & Lamar, 1912.

Newspapers

New Orleans Daily Picayune, 1878

New York Sun, 1872

Government Documents

Census of Arkansas County, Arkansas, 1850, 1860

Census of Jefferson County, Arkansas, 1860

Census of Ouachita County, Arkansas, 1860

United States Department of Commerce. *Historical Statistics of the United States*. Vol. 2. Washington, D.C.: Government Printing Office, 1975.

United States War Department. *War of the Rebellion: A Compilation of the Official Records of the Union and Confederate Armies*. 128 parts in 70 vols. Washington, D.C.: Government Printing Office, 1880–1901.

———. *Supplement to the Official Records of the Union and Confederate Armies*. Edited by Janet B. Hewett, Noah A. Trudeau, and Bryce A. Suderow. Part II. Vols. 1–   . Wilmington, N.C.: Broadfoot Publishing, 1994–   .

Secondary Sources
Books

Andreas, Alfred T. *History of Chicago*. Vol. 2. 1884. Reprint, New York: Arno Press, 1975.

Anstruther, Ian. *Dr. Livingstone, I Presume?* New York: E. P. Dutton, 1957.

Beatie, Russel H. *Saddles.* Norman: University of Oklahoma Press, 1981.

Bierman, John. *Dark Safari: The Life Behind the Legend of Henry Morton Stanley.* New York: Alfred A. Knopf, 1990.

Christovich, Mary Louise, Roulhac Toledano, Betty Swanson, and Pat Holder. *New Orleans Architecture.* Vol. 1. Gretna, La.: Pelican Publishing, 1972.

Confederate Soldiers, Sailors, and Civilians Who Died as Prisoners of War at Camp Douglas, Chicago, Ill., 1862–1865. Kalamazoo, Mich.: Edgar Gray, n.d.

Connelly, Thomas L. *Army of the Heartland: The Army of Tennessee, 1861–1862.* Baton Rouge: Louisiana State University Press, 1967.

Crute, Joseph H., Jr. *Confederate Staff Officers, 1861–1865.* Powhatan, Va.: Derwent Books, 1982.

Daniel, Larry J. *Shiloh: The Battle that Changed the Civil War.* New York: Simon & Schuster, 1997.

Dunlap, H. Jack. *American, British, and Continental Pepperbox Firearms.* Palo Alto, Cal.: Pacific Books, 1964.

Evans, Clement A., ed. *Confederate Military History.* Vol. 10. Atlanta: Confederate Publishing, 1899.

Farwell, Byron. *The Man Who Presumed.* New York: Norton, 1989.

Federal Writers Project, New Orleans. *New Orleans City Guide.* Boston: Houghton Mifflin, 1938.

George, Thomas. *The Birth, Boyhood, and Younger Days of Henry Stanley.* London: Roxburghen Press, 1895.

Gluckman, Arcadi. *United States Muskets, Rifles, and Carbines.* Buffalo: Otto Ulbrich, 1948.

Goodspeed, Weston. *Biographical and Historical Memoirs of Central Arkansas.* Chicago: Goodspeed Publishing, 1889.

———. *Biographical and Historical Memoirs of Eastern Arkansas.* Chicago: Goodspeed Publishing, 1890.

Hall, Richard. *Stanley: An Adventurer Explored.* Boston: Houghton Mifflin, 1975.

Heyl, Erik. *Early American Steamers.* 6 vols. Buffalo: n.p., 1969.

Hughes, Nathaniel C., Jr. *The Battle of Belmont: Grant Strikes South.* Chapel Hill: University of North Carolina Press, 1991

———. *General William J. Hardee: Old Reliable.* Baton Rouge: Louisiana State University Press, 1965.

Jones, Lucy M., and Ivor Wynne. *H. M. Stanley and Wales.* St. Asaph: H. M. Stanley Exhibition Committee, 1972.

Levy, George. *To Die in Chicago: Confederate Prisoners at Camp Douglas, 1862–65.* Gretna, La.: Pelican Publishing, 1999.

Lonn, Ella. *Foreigners in the Confederacy*. Chapel Hill: University of North Carolina Press, 1940.

McLynn, Frank J. *Stanley: The Making of an African Explorer*. Chelsea, Mich.: Scarborough House, 1990.

Mooney, James L., ed. *Dictionary of American Fighting Ships*. Washington, D.C.: Naval Historical Center, 1981.

Moorehead, Alan. *The White Nile*. New York: Harper & Brothers, 1960.

Morehead, Albert H., ed. *The Complete Hoyle*. Rev. ed. New York: Doubleday, 1991.

Neal, Diane, and Thomas W. Kremm. *The Lion of the South: General Thomas C. Hindman*. Macon, Ga.: Mercer University Press, 1993.

Parlett, David. *The Oxford Guide to Card Games*. New York: Oxford University Press, 1990.

Rowlands, Cadwalader. *H. M. Stanley: The Story of His Life*. London: n.p., 1872.

Scully, Arthur J. *James Dakin, Architect: His Career in New York and the South*. Baton Rouge: Louisiana State University Press, 1973.

Stephenson, Philip Daingerfield, *The Civil War Memoir of Philip Daingerfield Stephenson, D.D.* Edited by Nathaniel C. Hughes, Jr. 1995. Reprint, Baton Rouge: Louisiana State University Press, 1998.

Sword, Wiley. *Shiloh: Bloody April*. Dayton, Ohio: Morningside Bookshop, 1983.

Taylerson, A. W. F., R. A. N. Andrews, and J. Frith. *The Revolver, 1818–1865*. New York: Crown Publishers, 1968.

Wassermann, Jakob. *Bula Matari: Stanley, Conqueror of a Continent*. New York: Liveright, 1933.

Wilkinson, Frederick. *Small Arms*. New York: Hawthorn Books, 1965.

Wright, Marcus J. *Arkansas in the War, 1861–1865*. Edited by A. C. McGinnis. Batesville, Ark.: Independence County Historical Society, 1963.

Articles

Cross, Victoria. "The Goree Family." *Arkansas Historical Quarterly* 12 (summer 1953): 115–18.

Dillon, Catherine M. "From Wharf Waif to Knighthood." *Roosevelt Review* 7 (June 1944): 23, 27–33.

Hodges, T. L. "Possibilities for the Archaeologist and Historian in Eastern Arkansas." *Arkansas Historical Quarterly* 2 (June 1943): 141–63.

Kendall, John S. "Old New Orleans Houses and Some of the People Who Lived in Them." *Louisiana Historical Quarterly* 20 (July–September 1937): 794–820.

Laurie, Clayton D. "Two-Sided Adventure." *Civil War Times Illustrated* 24 (June 1985): 40–47.

Shuey, Mary Willis. "Stanley in New Orleans." *Southwest Review* 25 (1939–40): 378–93.

———. "Young Stanley; Arkansas Episode." *Southwest Review* 27 (winter 1944): 356–66.

Index